A/79/17

General Assembly
Official Records
Seventy-ninth Session
Supplement No. 17

Report of the United Nations Commission on International Trade Law

Fifty-seventh session
(24 June–12 July 2024)

United Nations • New York, 2024

Note

Symbols of United Nations documents are composed of letters combined with figures. Mention of such a symbol indicates a reference to a United Nations document.

Print ISNB: 978-92-1-003420-3
eSBN: 978-92-1-107039-2

Contents

I. Introduction

1. The present report of the United Nations Commission on International Trade Law (UNCITRAL) covers the fifty-seventh session of the Commission, held in New York from 24 June to 12 July 2024.

2. Pursuant to General Assembly resolution 2205 (XXI) of 17 December 1966, the present report is submitted to the General Assembly and is also submitted for comments to the United Nations Conference on Trade and Development (UNCTAD).

II. Organization of the session

A. Opening of the session

3. The fifty-seventh session of the Commission was opened by the Assistant Secretary-General for Legal Affairs, Mr. Stephen Mathias, on 24 June 2024.

B. Membership and attendance

4. The General Assembly, in its resolution 2205 (XXI), established the Commission with a membership of 29 States, elected by the Assembly. By its resolution 3108 (XXVIII) of 12 December 1973, the General Assembly increased the membership of the Commission from 29 to 36 States. By its resolution 57/20 of 19 November 2002, the General Assembly further increased the membership of the Commission from 36 States to 60 States. By its resolution 76/109 of 9 December 2021, the General Assembly increased the membership of the Commission from 60 to 70 States. Five additional members were elected during the seventy-sixth session of the General Assembly, with the remaining five additional members to be elected during the seventy-ninth session of the Assembly.

5. The current members of the Commission are the following States, whose term of office expires on the last day prior to the beginning of the annual session of the Commission in the year indicated:[1] Afghanistan (2028), Algeria (2025), Argentina (2028), Armenia (2028), Australia (2028), Austria (2028), Belarus (2028), Belgium (2025), Brazil (2028), Bulgaria (2028), Cameroon (2025), Canada (2025), Chile (2028), China (2025), Colombia (2028), Côte d'Ivoire (2025), Croatia (2025), Czechia (2028), Democratic Republic of the Congo (2028), Dominican Republic (2025), Ecuador (2025), Finland (2025), France (2025), Germany (2025), Ghana (2025), Greece (2028), Honduras (2025), Hungary (2025), India (2028), Indonesia (2025), Iran (Islamic Republic of) (2028), Iraq (2028), Israel (2028), Italy (2028), Japan (2025), Kenya (2028), Kuwait (2028), Malawi (2028), Malaysia (2025), Mali (2025), Mauritius (2028), Mexico (2025), Morocco (2028), Nigeria (2028), Panama (2028), Peru (2025), Poland (2028), Republic of Korea (2025), Russian Federation (2025), Saudi Arabia (2028), Singapore (2025), Somalia (2028), South Africa (2025), Spain (2028), Switzerland (2025), Thailand (2028), Türkiye (2028), Turkmenistan (2028), Uganda (2028), Ukraine (2025), United Kingdom of Great Britain and Northern Ireland (2025), United States of America (2028), Venezuela (Bolivarian Republic of) (2028), Viet Nam (2025) and Zimbabwe (2025).

[1] Pursuant to General Assembly resolution 2205 (XXI), the members of the Commission are elected for a term of six years. Of the current membership, 30 were elected by the Assembly on 17 December 2018, at its seventy-third session, 34 were elected by the Assembly on 15 March 2022, at its seventy-sixth session, and one was elected by the Assembly on 29 June 2022, at its seventy-sixth session. By its resolution 31/99, the Assembly altered the dates of commencement and termination of membership by deciding that members would take office at the beginning of the first day of the regular annual session of the Commission immediately following their election and that their terms of office would expire on the last day prior to the opening of the seventh regular annual session following their election.

6. With the exception of Afghanistan, Belgium, Cameroon, Croatia, Greece, Honduras, Malawi, Mali, Nigeria, Panama, Somalia, Turkmenistan and Uganda, all the members of the Commission were represented at the session.

7. The session was attended by observers from the following States: Costa Rica, Egypt, El Salvador, Equatorial Guinea, Guinea, Guinea-Bissau, Luxembourg, Namibia, Oman, Paraguay, Philippines, Qatar, Sierra Leone, Sri Lanka, Sweden, Uruguay and Zambia.

8. The session was also attended by observers from the European Union.

9. The session was also attended by observers from the following international organizations:

(a) United Nations system: International Monetary Fund and World Bank Group;

(b) Intergovernmental organizations: African Union, Asian-African Legal Consultative Organization (AALCO), Commonwealth Secretariat, Eurasian Economic Commission, International Institute for the Unification of Private Law (UNIDROIT), International Organization of la Francophonie and Permanent Court of Arbitration (PCA);

(c) Invited non-governmental organizations: Advisory Council of the United Nations Convention on Contracts for the International Sale of Goods, African Association of International Law, Beijing Arbitration Commission/Beijing International Arbitration Center, Center for International Commercial and Investment Arbitration, Centre for Legal, Economic and Political Studies (CEDEP) of Paraguay, China International Economic and Trade Arbitration Commission, China Society of Private International Law, Construction Industry Arbitration Council, Council of the Notariats of the European Union, European Law Institute, Inter-American Bar Association, International and Comparative Law Research Center, International Bar Association, International Chamber of Commerce, International Insolvency Institute, International Law Institute, International Union of Notaries, Islamic Chamber of Commerce, Industry and Agriculture, Latin American Group of Lawyers for International Trade Law, Miami International Arbitration Society, Moot Alumni Association, New York International Arbitration Center, New York State Bar Association, Nigerian Institute of Chartered Arbitrators, Shanghai Arbitration Commission, Shenzhen Court of International Arbitration, Singapore International Arbitration Centre and United States Council for International Business.

10. The Commission welcomed the participation of international non-governmental organizations with expertise in the major items on the agenda. Their participation was crucial for the quality of texts formulated by the Commission, and the Commission requested the secretariat to continue to invite such organizations to its sessions.

C. Election of officers

11. The Commission elected the following officers:

Chair:	Vilawan Mangklatanakul (Thailand)
Vice-Chairs:	Alex Ivanco (Czechia) Andrés Jana (Chile) Shane Spelliscy (Canada)
Rapporteur:	Siaka Traore (Côte d'Ivoire)

D. Agenda

12. The agenda of the fifty-seventh session of the Commission as contained in the note by the Secretariat (A/CN.9/1157/Rev.1) was adopted by the Commission at its 1206th meeting, on 24 June 2024, as follows:

1. Opening of the session.
2. Election of officers.
3. Adoption of the agenda.
4. Consideration of the draft model law on warehouse receipts and guide to enactment.
5. Coordination and cooperation.
6. Secretariat reports on non-legislative activities:
   (a) Overview of non-legislative activities;
   (b) Status and promotion of UNCITRAL legal texts;
   (c) Relevant General Assembly resolutions;
   (d) Current role of UNCITRAL in promoting the rule of law;
   (e) Bibliography of recent writings related to the work of UNCITRAL.
7. Progress reports of working groups.
8. Work programme of the Commission:
   (a) Consideration of climate change mitigation, adaptation and resilience;
   (b) Consideration of secured transactions using new types of assets and their treatment under the UNCITRAL Model Law on Secured Transactions;
   (c) Methods of work, including streamlining General Assembly resolutions on UNCITRAL annual reports;
   (d) Consideration of dispute resolution in the digital economy;
   (e) Consideration of legal issues relating to the use of distributed ledger technology in trade;
   (f) Consideration of any additional topics for possible future work by UNCITRAL.
9. Consideration of draft model clauses on specialized express dispute resolution.
10. Consideration of texts prepared in the context of investor-State dispute settlement reform:
    (a) Consideration of the draft statute of an advisory centre on international investment dispute resolution;
    (b) Consideration of the draft toolkit on dispute prevention and mitigation.
11. Consideration of the draft provisions on automated contracting and guide to enactment.
12. Date and place of future meetings.

13. Other business:

(a) Evaluation of the role of the UNCITRAL secretariat in facilitating the work of the Commission;

(b) Other matters.

14. Adoption of the report of the Commission.

E. Adoption of the report

13. The Commission adopted the present report by consensus at its 1215th meeting, on 28 June 2024, at its 1223rd meeting, on 5 July 2024, and at its 1233rd meeting, on 12 July 2024.

III. Summary of the work of the Commission at its fifty-seventh session

14. With respect to agenda item 4 (Consideration of the draft model law on warehouse receipts and guide to enactment), the Commission finalized and adopted the UNCITRAL-UNIDROIT Model Law on Warehouse Receipts, which is reproduced in annex I to the present report, and approved in principle the draft guide to enactment.

15. With respect to agenda item 5 (Coordination and cooperation), the Commission took note of the notes by the Secretariat on coordination activities and on international governmental and non-governmental organizations invited to sessions of UNCITRAL and its working groups, as well as the reports by AALCO, the Organization for the Harmonization of Business Law in Africa (OHADA), PCA and UNIDROIT.

16. With respect to agenda item 6 (Secretariat reports on non-legislative activities), the Commission took note of the notes by the Secretariat concerning non-legislative activities, and more specifically:

(a) The Commission authorized the secretariat to publish the updated edition of the *UNCITRAL Digest of Case Law on the Model Law on International Commercial Arbitration* and the analytical compilation of case law on the Convention on the Limitation Period in the International Sale of Goods (the 1974 Limitation Convention), and to make them generally known and available;

(b) The Commission authorized the secretariat to pursue its consultations with database and search engine platforms with a view to outsourcing the upgrading of the Case Law on UNCITRAL Texts (CLOUT) database;

(c) The Commission decided to recommend to the General Assembly that it request the Secretary-General to continue to operate, through the secretariat of the Commission, the transparency repository in accordance with article 8 of the UNCITRAL Rules on Transparency in Treaty-based Investor-State Arbitration as a continuation of the project until the end of 2027, subject to funding;

(d) The Commission authorized the secretariat to publish the updated publication *A Guide to UNCITRAL: Basic Facts about the United Nations Commission on International Trade Law* and to make it generally known and available;

(e) The Commission renewed its appeal to Governments, the relevant bodies of the United Nations system, organizations, institutions and individuals to make voluntary contributions to the trust fund for UNCITRAL symposiums and the trust fund established to provide travel assistance to developing countries that are members of UNCITRAL and contributions for the financing of special projects and to otherwise assist the secretariat in carrying out its non-legislative activities, in particular technical cooperation and assistance activities in developing countries, and recalled the relevance of the United Nations Pledging Conference for Development Activities in that context.

17. With respect to agenda item 7 (Progress reports of working groups), the Commission took note of the progress report of Working Group III (Investor-State Dispute Settlement Reform), Working Group IV (Electronic Commerce), Working Group V (Insolvency Law) and Working Group VI (Negotiable Cargo Documents). The Commission expressed its satisfaction with the progress made by those working groups. With regard to the progress report of Working Group V, the Commission requested the secretariat to update the *UNCITRAL Practice Guide on Cross-Border Insolvency Cooperation*, resources permitting and in consultation with relevant experts, and to present a revised text for review by the Working Group before transmitting it to the Commission for consideration and finalization. The work of Working Group I (Warehouse Receipts) and Working Group II (Dispute Settlement) was considered under agenda items 4 and 9.

18. With respect to agenda item 8 (Work programme of the Commission), the Commission:

(a) Confirmed the programme of current legislative activities carried out by its Working Groups III, IV, V and VI;

(b) Mandated Working Group II to work on the recognition and enforcement of electronic arbitral awards and, subsequently, on electronic notices;

(c) Requested the secretariat to circulate the UNCITRAL-UNIDROIT study on the legal nature of verified carbon credits issued by independent carbon standard setters to all States Members of the United Nations and give them sufficient time to provide the secretariat with their technical and editorial comments, and agreed to hold a further discussion on the study during its fifty-eighth session;

(d) Requested the secretariat to organize a two-day colloquium in a hybrid format, with a focus on the relevance of UNCITRAL instruments to climate action, utilizing conference time tentatively allocated to Working Group I in the second half of 2024;

(e) Requested the secretariat to continue and finalize its work on a guidance document on legal issues relating to the use of distributed ledger systems in trade, within existing resources, and in cooperation with other organizations, as appropriate;

(f) Requested the secretariat to take stock of legislative developments related to new types of assets and the secured transaction laws of States to examine how the UNCITRAL Model Law on Secured Transactions had been implemented, and to organize a two- or three-day colloquium in a hybrid format to clarify and refine various aspects of possible future work in the area, utilizing conference time tentatively allocated to Working Group I in the first half of 2025;

(g) Requested the secretariat to conduct a stocktaking exercise to examine all UNCITRAL texts that referred to electronic aspects, including a survey of the incorporation by States of UNCITRAL texts on electronic commerce into their domestic legislation and the inclusion of such texts in international commitments concerning paperless trade. The secretariat was further requested to coordinate with other relevant organizations in the field of paperless trade.

19. Also with respect to agenda item 8 (Work programme of the Commission), under the subitem "Methods of work, including streamlining General Assembly resolutions on UNCITRAL annual reports", the Commission noted the outcome of the informal consultations on streamlining future UNCITRAL omnibus resolutions and requested that the secretariat continue to facilitate an open and flexible intersessional consultative process led in Vienna among States Members of the United Nations, involving not only delegates of Vienna-based Permanent Missions but also UNCITRAL focal points of member and observer States, with a view to preparing an UNCITRAL omnibus resolution reflecting some of the guiding principles in 2024.

20. With respect to agenda item 9 (Consideration of draft model clauses on specialized express dispute resolution), the Commission finalized and adopted the UNCITRAL Model Clauses on Specialized Express Dispute Resolution, which are reproduced in annex II to the present report, and approved in principle the draft explanatory notes.

21. With respect to agenda item 10 (Consideration of texts prepared in the context of investor-State dispute settlement reform), the Commission finalized and adopted in principle the Statute of the Advisory Centre on International Investment Dispute Resolution, which is reproduced in annex III to the present report, and recommended that all States and regional economic integration organizations take part in the preparatory work to operationalize the Advisory Centre on International Investment Dispute Resolution.

22. With respect to agenda item 11 (Consideration of the draft provisions on automated contracting and guide to enactment), the Commission finalized and adopted the UNCITRAL Model Law on Automated Contracting, which is reproduced in annex IV to the present report, and approved in principle the draft guide to enactment.

23. With respect to agenda item 12 (Date and place of future meetings), the Commission approved the holding of its fifty-eighth session in Vienna, from 7 to 25 July 2025, and the schedule for working group sessions to be held in the second half of 2024 and first half of 2025.

IV. Consideration of the UNCITRAL-UNIDROIT Model Law on Warehouse Receipts and guide to enactment

A. Introduction

24. The Commission recalled that, at its forty-ninth session, in 2016, it had decided to place the topic of warehouse receipt financing on its future work programme.[2] The Commission also recalled that, following the preparatory phase, it had agreed, at its fifty-third session, in 2020, to carry out the project jointly with UNIDROIT,[3] and that the joint UNIDROIT-UNCITRAL Working Group on a Model Law on Warehouse Receipts had held six sessions, following which a draft model law (A/CN.9/1152) had been transmitted to UNCITRAL by the UNIDROIT Governing Council, at its 102nd session (Rome, 10–12 May 2023) for State negotiations and completion.[4]

25. Following the decision by the Commission, at its fifty-sixth session, in 2023, to refer the draft model law on warehouse receipts to Working Group I,[5] the Working Group had completed two readings of the draft model law on warehouse receipts, at its fortieth session (Vienna, 25–29 September 2023) (A/CN.9/1158) and its forty-first session (New York, 5–9 February 2024) (A/CN.9/1165).

26. At the present session, the Commission considered the text of the draft model law on warehouse receipts (A/CN.9/1182), as it had emerged from the deliberations of the Working Group at its forty-first session, the draft guide to enactment thereto (A/CN.9/1183), as well as a compilation of comments submitted by States on the draft model law (A/CN.9/1188 and A/CN.9/1188/Add.1), which had been circulated prior to the session in accordance with UNCITRAL practice.

27. The following paragraphs summarize the deliberations of the Commission and the amendments agreed to the draft model law. Provisions of the draft model law not referred to below were approved by the Commission as they appear in document

[2] *Official Records of the General Assembly, Seventy-first Session, Supplement No. 17* (A/71/17), para. 125.

[3] Ibid., *Seventy-fifth Session, Supplement No. 17* (A/75/17), part two, para. 61.

[4] Ibid., *Seventy-eighth Session, Supplement No. 17* (A/78/17), para. 177.

[5] Ibid., paras. 22 (b) and 177.

A/CN.9/1182, subject to stylistic and linguistic adjustments that the secretariat was requested to make to ensure consistency in the text of the model law and conformity with United Nations editorial guidelines and official style.

B. Consideration of the draft model law

Chapter I. Scope and general provisions

Article 2. Definitions

28. Different preferences were expressed as to which variant of the definition of "holder" should be retained in paragraph 3, and on the drafting of that definition. Variant 1 was found by some to be more concise and clearer, whereas variant 2 was preferred by others because they felt that it better reflected the medium-neutral approach adopted by the Working Group. In response to a suggestion to retain both variants, the Commission noted that UNCITRAL texts rarely used variants and that they were used only to accommodate substantive differences in law. After discussion, the Commission decided to retain variant 2, reversing the order of the qualifiers in subparagraphs (a) (i) and (a) (ii) and subparagraphs (b) (i) and (b) (ii).

Article 3. Party autonomy

29. It was noted that the title of article 3 did not accurately reflect the content of that article, which in fact excluded party autonomy. It was suggested that article 3 should therefore be deleted or, alternatively, qualified by a reference to provisions that could be derogated from or varied. In response, it was recalled that the Working Group had not been able to identify any such provisions. The view was expressed that the identification of such provisions could be left to the implementing State. After discussion, the Commission decided to retain article 3 but to change its title to "Non-derogation".

Chapter II. Issuance and contents of a warehouse receipt; alteration and replacement

30. A suggestion was made to replace the words "alteration and replacement" with "replacement and change of medium" to better reflect the contents of chapter II. The Commission agreed to revise the title of chapter II accordingly.

Article 5. Obligation to issue a warehouse receipt

31. The Commission considered a suggestion to oblige warehouse operators who met certain requirements, to be specified by the enacting State in relevant laws and regulations, to issue warehouse receipts upon request by the depositor. In that connection, the question was raised as to whether the obligation to issue a warehouse receipt was absolute or arose only if established by the storage agreement. In response, it was noted that the model law acknowledged the existence of different business models of commodities storage, not all of which relied on the issuance of warehouse receipts. Depositors would in practice choose warehouse operators for various reasons, including whether or not they issued warehouse receipts, and, if so, under what conditions. The model law applied to warehouse receipts rather than storage agreements, but warehouse operators who offered to issue warehouse receipts would be obliged to issue warehouse receipts, upon request by the depositor, subject to the conditions set forth in the storage agreement (cost, contents liability, etc.). The Commission agreed to retain the article as drafted and to expand the explanations in the draft guide to enactment accordingly (for instance, para. 87 of the draft guide to enactment).

Article 6. Electronic warehouse receipt

32. It was indicated that the formulation of the chapeau of article 6 was inadequate, since the system employed to manage the electronic warehouse receipt, rather than

the receipt itself, should use a reliable method to pursue the functions listed in subparagraphs (a), (b) and (c) of paragraph 1. Alternative drafting suggestions were made. After discussion, the Commission agreed to replace the chapeau of article 6 with the following wording: "For the issuance and use of an electronic warehouse receipt, a reliable method shall be used:".

33. For purposes of internal consistency between paragraphs 1 (b) and 2, as well as coherence with previous UNCITRAL texts on electronic commerce, the Commission agreed to refer to "effect or validity" in both paragraphs.

Article 8. Representations by the depositor

34. The Commission recalled that the Working Group had agreed to clarify in the guide to enactment that when the depositor requested the issuance of a warehouse receipt, those representations were deemed to be made by operation of law, without the need for any additional formalities or declarations from the depositor (A/CN.9/1165, para. 39 (d)). The Commission requested the secretariat to revise the draft guide to enactment accordingly.

Article 9. Incorporation of storage agreement in the warehouse receipt

35. The Commission agreed to replace the phrase "shall be made available on request by the current holder to potential transferees" in paragraph 1 with the phrase "shall be made available to potential transferees upon request by the current holder". The Commission also agreed to delete the words "any person who becomes" and "or 16" in paragraph 2.

Article 10. Information to be included in a warehouse receipt

36. In respect of paragraph 2, it was explained that while any missing information would not affect the validity of the warehouse receipt, the requirements set out in article 1, paragraph 2, must be met for a document or record to be considered a warehouse receipt.

37. Divergent views were expressed on the presumption rule in paragraph 3. One view was that it was preferable not to promote the use of bearer instruments and to include a presumption rule in favour of non-negotiable warehouse receipts in the absence of any indication as to negotiability. Another view was that it was preferable to include a presumption rule in favour of negotiable warehouse receipts. It was pointed out that the wording of paragraph 3 reflected the decision of the Working Group at its fortieth session (A/CN.9/1158, para. 49). A third view was that it was preferable to include a conclusive presumption in favour of negotiable warehouse receipts. Such a presumption would not be rebuttable. After deliberation, the Commission agreed to retain the current wording.

Article 11. Additional information that may be included in a warehouse receipt

38. A suggestion was made to include a reference to information on the shelf life of perishable goods in paragraph 1 (c). In response, it was noted that it would be difficult to provide that information with sufficient clarity and objectivity (A/CN.9/1158, paras. 40 and 41).

39. In response to a query concerning the title to commingled goods, it was explained that depositors would share the title pro rata.

Article 13. Loss or destruction of a warehouse receipt

40. In response to a question about whether evidence of loss must be provided, it was explained that the provision did not establish any standard of proof but deferred to domestic law.

41. With regard to paragraph 1 (d), the Commission agreed to delete the word "reasonably" given that the chapeau already contained reference to reasonable

requirements. The Commission also agreed to delete the words within the first set of square brackets and retain the phrase "unless the storage agreement provides otherwise" without square brackets, noting that the parties should be allowed to derogate from the requirement in subparagraph (d).

42. With regard to paragraph 5, the Commission agreed to replace the words "other laws" with "other law" for consistency.

Article 14. Change of medium of a warehouse receipt

43. A question was raised as to how information in a paper document would be recorded in an electronic warehouse receipt. In response, reference was made to the integrity requirement set out in article 6, paragraph 2. The Commission agreed to clarify that issue in the guide to enactment.

44. The Commission agreed to revise article 14, paragraph 2, along the following lines: "At the time of the change of medium, the warehouse operator shall ensure that the warehouse receipt, in its previous medium, becomes inoperative and ceases to have any effect or validity."

Chapter III. Transfers and other dealings in negotiable warehouse receipts

45. A suggestion was made to provide for the subsidiary application of the Convention providing a Uniform Law for Bills of Exchange and Promissory Notes to matters not expressly addressed in chapter III of the model law. In response, it was noted that the Convention did not enjoy universal application and that, even in States parties to the Convention, it was generally accepted that warehouse receipts and other documents of title, such as bills of lading, were intrinsically connected to the underlying transaction and, therefore, were not regarded as abstract negotiable instruments, unlike bills of exchange and promissory notes. For that reason, only certain provisions of the Convention could provide useful guidance in interpreting chapter III.

Article 15. Transfer of a negotiable warehouse receipt

46. Views were expressed in favour of retaining the concept of endorsement, given that it would be useful in the digital world as it clearly identified the parties involved in a transfer and made it possible to easily track a chain of transfers regardless of the technology used. It was pointed out that the substantive law for paper and electronic warehouse receipts would be different if endorsement was not required for electronic warehouse receipts, which would not be consistent with the medium-neutral approach adopted by the model law.

47. A proposal was made to revise paragraph 2 and introduce a new paragraph 3 as follows:

"2. An electronic negotiable warehouse receipt may be transferred:

(a) By endorsement and transfer of control, if it is issued or endorsed to the order of the person transferring it; or

(b) By transfer of control, if:

(i) It is issued to bearer; or

(ii) It is endorsed in blank or to bearer.

"3. For the purpose of paragraph 2, the requirements for the endorsement of an electronic warehouse receipt are met if the information required for the endorsement:

(a) Is included in the electronic warehouse receipt;

(b) Is accessible so as to be usable for subsequent reference; and

(c) Is signed."

48. It was explained that the drafting proposal, which was based on article 15 of the UNCITRAL Model Law on Electronic Transferable Records,[6] would enable the endorsement of electronic warehouse receipts. In response, it was noted that article 15 of the UNCITRAL Model Law on Electronic Transferable Records was based on a functional equivalence approach that enabled endorsement where substantive law already required or permitted it. However, the endorsement of warehouse receipts had only a security function, which in most cases was achieved with annotation in registries, and the endorser was not held liable for the performance of the warehouse operator (see also art. 20). For that reason, the Working Group had decided not to refer to the endorsement of electronic warehouse receipts (A/CN.9/1165, para. 60). After discussion, the Commission decided to retain the current wording of the draft article.

Article 16. Rights of a transferee generally

49. The view was expressed that the provision should be revised to include one more option to better reflect the two different options in article 18, namely, (a) a protected holder of a negotiable warehouse receipt would acquire ownership of the goods covered by the receipt, and (b) a protected holder of a negotiable warehouse receipt would acquire such rights to the goods as it would acquire by the transfer of physical possession of the goods under other law.

50. The Commission heard a proposal to introduce a second option for paragraph 1 that would read:

"A person to whom a negotiable warehouse receipt has been transferred acquires:

(a) The benefit of the obligation of the warehouse operator to hold and deliver the goods in accordance with the terms of the receipt;

(b) Such rights to the receipt as the transferor was able to convey; and

(c) Such rights to the goods as it would acquire by the transfer of physical possession of the goods under other law and as the transferor was able to convey."

51. In response, it was indicated that article 16 was flexible in accommodating differences in property law and did not affect the rights transferred to a protected holder under article 18. After discussion, the Commission decided to retain the current wording of the draft article and to explain in the guide to enactment how differences in property law could be accommodated under article 16.

Article 18. Rights of a protected holder of a negotiable warehouse receipt

52. A suggestion was made to add to option 2, paragraph 1 (b), a provision preserving any claim or defence available to the warehouse operator concerning the validity of statements made in the warehouse receipt or that the warehouse operator was directly entitled to invoke against the holder. In response, it was noted that the draft article shielded the protected holder against any personal defences that the warehouse operator might enforce against the depositor (see also A/CN.9/1158, paras. 75 and 76). However, the article left intact any remedies that the warehouse operator might have against the depositor (for instance, arising from duress or fraud). After discussion, the Commission decided to retain the current wording of the draft article.

Article 21. Limited representation by intermediaries

53. A suggestion to insert a requirement to disclose the existence of an agency and to clarify the rights of the agent, inspired by article 18 of the Convention providing a Uniform Law for Bills of Exchange and Promissory Notes, did not receive support.

---

[6] Ibid., *Seventy-second Session, Supplement No. 17* (A/72/17), annex I.

Chapter IV. Rights and obligations of the warehouse operator

Article 23. Duty of care

54. It was suggested that article 23 should include a reference to the contractual duty of care specified in the warehouse receipt, as the primary parameter for the warehouse operator's duty of care. In response, it was noted that the draft article did not prevent the parties from providing contractually for the operator's duty of care, or even raise its level. In fact, the article assumed that such provisions would normally exist. Nevertheless, in the interest of protecting depositors and holders, article 23 contained a statutory duty of care and provided a mandatory baseline for any contractual agreement.

55. A suggestion was made to refer to "operator" instead of "owner" in paragraph 1 because the owner had no duty of care and was entitled to destroy the goods. For that reason, it was preferable to refer to industry standards. After recalling the Working Group discussions (A/CN.9/1165, paras. 73 and 75), the Commission agreed to replace the words "owner of goods of that type" with "warehouse operator storing goods of that type".

Article 25. Lien of the warehouse operator

56. The Commission agreed to replace the words "as permitted by" with "pursuant to" in paragraph 4.

57. The Commission agreed to clarify in the guide to enactment that the lien would only cover outstanding charges and expenses.

Article 28. Split warehouse receipt

58. The Commission agreed to delete the phrase in the first set of square brackets and remove the square brackets around the phrase in the second set of square brackets in paragraph 1.

59. The Commission agreed to replace the word "delivery" with "issuance" in paragraph 2 to avoid the possible simultaneous circulation of multiple warehouse receipts relating to the same goods and to accommodate the use of electronic warehouse receipts.

60. In response to a query regarding the date of issuance of split warehouse receipts, the Commission confirmed that the subsequent issuance of split warehouse receipts would not affect the security interests in the original warehouse receipt, which would continue to attach to the entirety of the goods covered by the split receipts.

Article 29. Excuses from delivery obligation

61. The view was expressed that the article dealt with two different types of circumstances under which the warehouse operator was relieved of its obligation to deliver the goods: some related to a permanent impediment or impossibility, as in the case of subparagraphs (a) and (b), whereas subparagraph (c) (and possibly also (d), depending on whether the judicial decision was an interim measure or a final judgment) related to a temporary impediment. It was argued that the word "relieved" in the chapeau of article 29 denoted a definite exoneration and was not appropriate in all instances. The notion of "competing claims" was also felt to be vague, and a reference to conflicting delivery instructions would be preferable. Some delegations suggested that additional guidance could be provided on the resolution of competing claims by judicial or other means, including at the warehouse operator's initiative and risk. In response, it was questioned whether that level of detail was needed.

62. A suggestion was made to split article 29 into two paragraphs listing the permanent impediments in subparagraphs (a), (b) and (d) to the extent that the court order was final; and the temporary impediments in subparagraphs (c) and (d) to the extent that the court order was temporary.

63. The view was expressed that subparagraph (c) was unnecessary since subparagraph (d) already covered situations in which a conflict of claims became the object of a court order, whereas subparagraph (c) offered no guidance as to how a conflict might be resolved and how long the suspension of the delivery obligation would last. In response, it was indicated that subparagraph (c) provided useful guidance on a delicate matter that could expose the warehouse operator to significant risk.

64. After deliberation, the Commission agreed to delete subparagraph (c) and to clarify in the guide to enactment that the warehouse operator had different options, which included judicial remedies and the exercise of discretion in: (a) assessing the merits of competing delivery instructions; and (b) delivering the goods, at its own risk, to the claimant believed to have a better title. The Commission also agreed that the guide to enactment should clarify the permanent or temporary nature of the impediments in article 29.

65. A suggestion to add a provision on exoneration from the obligation of the warehouse operator to deliver the goods in the event of the disposal of hazardous goods under certain circumstances did not receive support. It was recalled that article 30, paragraph 4, dealt with that situation.

Article 30. Termination of storage by the warehouse operator

66. The Commission agreed to: (a) reverse the order of paragraphs 2 and 3 to clarify that the current paragraph 2 applied to any notice required under the article, whether or not any person with an interest in the goods was known; (b) in current paragraph 2, replace the words "by paragraph 1" with "under this article"; and (c) in current paragraph 3, replace the words "are about to" with "will".

67. The Commission accepted a proposal to replace the words "did not have knowledge" with "neither knew nor ought to have known" in paragraph 4, to ensure that a warehouse operator could not dispose unilaterally of hazardous goods that had been accepted in storage. It was indicated that the suggested redraft could facilitate the provision of evidence of the lack of knowledge of the hazardous nature of the goods.

68. The Commission considered at length the meaning of the words "public sale" and "private sale" and the requirement of commercial reasonableness in the context of the draft provision. It was noted that the reference to domestic laws governing the conduct of public sales seemed to imply that those were sales under judicial authority, whereas private sales were conducted by the warehouse operator. If that was indeed the intention, the use of the words "judicial" or "by the warehouse operator" would be a clearer way of expressing that dichotomy. The terms currently used, however, seemed to be inspired by the law of other jurisdictions where both "public" and "private" sales were conducted by the warehouse operator, rather than under judicial authority, but were subject to extensive requirements of commercial reasonableness, which the draft model law could not reproduce. The current wording was not only misleading, as it used terms to which different legal systems attached different meanings, but also inappropriate in the context because, for instance, sales conducted under any State supervision pursuant to specific legislation could be presumed to meet a standard of commercial reasonability.

69. Having considered the various views, the Commission agreed to delete "by public sale, according to [*relevant law on public sale as specified by the enacting State*], or private sale" in paragraph 1 (b) so that the provision would refer only to the warehouse operators' right to sell the goods "in any commercially reasonable manner". The guide to enactment should explain the variety of methods by which warehouse operators might be authorized to sell the goods under domestic laws and explain that the commercial reasonableness standard would need to be considered in domestic contexts.

Chapter V. Pledge bonds

Article 31. Scope of provisions on pledge bonds

70. There was not sufficient support for a suggestion to delete the text in the footnote to the title of chapter V, or for a suggestion to reverse the order of draft articles 31 and 32.

Article 32. Issuance and form of a pledge bond

71. The Commission accepted a proposal to delete the word "possessory" in paragraph 1 (b) in order to facilitate understanding of the model law in some legal systems. However, the intention was not to remove the distinction made between possessory and non-possessory security interests in the *UNCITRAL Legislative Guide on Secured Transactions*.[7]

72. The Commission agreed to replace the text of paragraph 2 with the alternative text proposed in footnote 8.

73. The Commission also agreed to adopt variant 2 of paragraph 3 in order to align the provision with the revised definition of "holder" of a warehouse receipt in article 2 and to redraft subparagraphs (a) and (b) to mirror paragraph 3 (b) of article 2, including subparagraphs (a) (i) and (ii) and (b) (i) and (ii).

Article 35. Rights and obligations of the warehouse operator

74. The Commission accepted a suggestion to delete the words "pursuant to article 34, paragraph 1" from paragraph 1, as they were unnecessary.

75. The view was expressed that the article could be split into two articles, as it dealt with separate matters: paragraph 1 dealt with split warehouse receipts, whereas paragraphs 2 and 3 dealt with the delivery of the goods.

76. The Commission accepted, however, the opposing view that the entire article was concerned with rights and obligations of the warehouse operator and adopted it with the amendment mentioned in paragraph 74 above.

C. Consideration of the draft guide to enactment

77. The Commission proceeded to consider the text of the draft guide to enactment and requested the secretariat to make the following changes, in addition to the adjustments consequential to the Commission's deliberations on the text of the model law:

(a) Revise the text to ensure that whenever reference was made to both paper and electronic warehouse receipts, the electronic version was mentioned first;

(b) In the first bullet point in paragraph 7, replace the word "commodity" with "goods", and add a reference to the requirement that the warehouse receipt be surrendered;

(c) In paragraph 34, replace the words "While the Model Law encompasses both negotiable and non-negotiable warehouse receipts, emphasis is placed on negotiable warehouse receipts, since non-negotiable warehouse receipts are more likely to be issued" with "While recognizing that non-negotiable warehouse receipts are widely used, emphasis is placed on negotiable warehouse receipts in view of the need to protect the interest of holders. Moreover, non-negotiable warehouse receipts are often issued …";

(d) In paragraph 58, replace "disproportionate" with "special";

[7] United Nations publication, Sales No. E.09.V.12.

(e) In paragraph 69, add a bullet point as follows: "The law applicable to the creation, third-party effectiveness, priority and enforcement of security rights in documents of title, including warehouse receipts.";

(f) In paragraph 78, delete the text after the word "delivery";

(g) In paragraph 80, add a reference to the need for the issuer to indicate clearly when a warehouse receipt was non-negotiable, for instance by using language prohibiting its transfer or equivalent formulations (A/CN.9/1165, para. 20);

(h) In paragraph 84, indicate that article 4 did not mean that an intermediary was prevented by article 21 from making additional representations and that a transferor was prevented by article 22 from guaranteeing the performance by the warehouse operator of its obligations (A/CN.9/1165, para. 29);

(i) In paragraph 91, clarify that representations were deemed to be made by operation of law (see para. 34);

(j) In paragraph 94, clarify that liability was a consequence of the misrepresentations made by the depositor and did not arise from article 8;

(k) In paragraph 100, explain how the presumption of negotiability would operate in practice (see para. 37);

(l) In paragraph 105, indicate that warehouse operators should not make excessive use of the provision as otherwise, the warehouse receipt would have limited commercial value (see also A/CN.9/1165, para. 51);

(m) At the end of paragraph 130, add the words "under other law";

(n) In paragraph 135, place references to UNCITRAL and UNIDROIT documents in the footnote;

(o) In paragraph 139, replace the fifth sentence with the following wording: "The transferee will not acquire any rights in goods if the warehouse receipt is a forgery, and the transferee's position will be prejudiced if the second representation is incorrect.";

(p) In paragraph 160, clarify that the last sentence did not refer to a condition under the model law but to a possible requirement of the warehouse operator based on commercial considerations;

(q) In paragraph 163, insert the words "temporarily suspended or" before "excused";

(r) In paragraph 175, replace the fourth sentence as follows: "In this way, the dual warehouse receipt system allows separate circulation of goods and secured credit in commodity trade financing."; and in the fifth sentence, replace "also" with "instead";

(s) In paragraphs 176 and 177, replace references to the notion of "detachability" with references to "separability", and remove all quotation marks around words;

(t) In section D of part IV, on complementary legislation, clarify the relationship between the central registry of warehouse receipts and the central registry of security interests, as foreseen in the UNCITRAL Model Law on Secured Transactions.

D. Adoption of the UNCITRAL-UNIDROIT Model Law on Warehouse Receipts

78. After completing its consideration of the text of the draft UNCITRAL-UNIDROIT model law on warehouse receipts (A/CN.9/1182) and the accompanying

draft guide to enactment (A/CN.9/1183), the Commission adopted by consensus the following decision at its 1210th meeting, on 26 June 2024:

"*The United Nations Commission on International Trade Law*,

"*Recalling* its mandate under General Assembly resolution 2205 (XXI) of 17 December 1966 to further the progressive harmonization and unification of the law of international trade and in that respect to bear in mind the interests of all peoples, in particular those of developing countries, in the extensive development of international trade,

"*Recalling also* its decision at the forty-ninth session, in 2016, to place the topic of warehouse receipt financing on its future work programme,[8] its decision at the fifty-third session, in 2020, that work towards the development of a model law on the private law aspects of warehouse receipts would be carried out jointly with the International Institute for the Unification of Private Law, and that the final text would bear the names of both organizations in recognition of their close cooperation,[9] and its decision at the fifty-sixth session, in 2023, to refer the draft model law on warehouse receipts developed by the joint UNIDROIT-UNCITRAL Working Group on a Model Law on Warehouse Receipts to Working Group I (Warehouse Receipts),[10]

"*Convinced* that the enactment of a modern warehouse receipts law supporting the issuance and transfer of electronic and paper-based receipts alike could facilitate commercial transactions that involve stored goods, including as collateral for financing, especially in least developed and developing countries,

"*Believing* that such a modern warehouse receipts law could also contribute to promoting short-term financing in the agricultural sector, thus facilitating access to credit and reducing the cost of financing for farmers, and attracting private sector investments to the agricultural sector,

"*Expecting* that the harmonization of warehouse receipt laws could aid the formation of regional and international commodities markets,

"*Noting* that the improved ability of farmers and countries to grow and store crops and other agricultural products has the potential to increase global food production and assist in overcoming the food security challenge, thus contributing to the achievement of Sustainable Development Goal 2 (End hunger, achieve food security and improved nutrition and promote sustainable agriculture),

"*Having considered*, at its fifty-seventh session, in 2024, a draft model law on warehouse receipts[11] and an accompanying guide to enactment,[12] prepared by Working Group I, together with comments on the draft received from Governments,[13]

"*Expressing* its appreciation to Working Group I and to the joint UNIDROIT-UNCITRAL Working Group for their work in developing the draft UNCITRAL-UNIDROIT model law on warehouse receipts,

"1. *Adopts* the UNCITRAL-UNIDROIT Model Law on Warehouse Receipts, as contained in annex I to the report of the United Nations Commission on International Trade Law on the work of its fifty-seventh session;[14]

"2. *Approves* in principle the draft guide to enactment of the UNCITRAL-UNIDROIT Model Law on Warehouse Receipts, and requests the secretariat to

[8] *Official Records of the General Assembly, Seventy-first Session, Supplement No. 17* (A/71/17), para. 125.
[9] Ibid., *Seventy-fifth Session, Supplement No. 17* (A/75/17), part two, para. 61.
[10] Ibid., *Seventy-eighth Session, Supplement No. 17* (A/78/17), para. 22 (b).
[11] A/CN.9/1182.
[12] A/CN.9/1183.
[13] A/CN.9/1188.
[14] *Official Records of the General Assembly, Seventy-ninth Session, Supplement No. 17* (A/79/17), annex I.

finalize it by reflecting deliberations and decisions at the fifty-seventh session of the Commission;

"3. *Requests* the Secretary-General to publish the UNCITRAL-UNIDROIT Model Law on Warehouse Receipts together with a guide to enactment, including electronically, in the six official languages of the United Nations, and to disseminate it broadly to Governments and other interested bodies;

"4. *Recommends* that all States give favourable consideration to the UNCITRAL-UNIDROIT Model Law on Warehouse Receipts when revising or adopting legislation relevant to warehouse receipts, and invites States that have used the Model Law to advise the Commission accordingly."

V. Consideration of the UNCITRAL Model Clauses on Specialized Express Dispute Resolution with accompanying explanatory notes

A. Introduction

79. The Commission recalled that, at its fifty-fifth session, in 2022, it had entrusted Working Group II with considering the topics of technology-related dispute resolution and adjudication jointly, and with considering ways to further accelerate the resolution of disputes. It had been agreed that the work should build on the UNCITRAL Expedited Arbitration Rules and that the model provisions, clauses or other forms of legislative or non-legislative text could be prepared on matters such as shorter time frames, the appointment of experts and/or neutrals, confidentiality and the legal nature of the outcome of the proceedings, all of which would allow disputing parties to tailor the proceedings to their needs to further expedite them.[15]

80. The Commission noted that Working Group II, at its seventy-ninth session, had concluded its preparation of the draft model clauses and requested the secretariat to prepare a revised version with the accompanying explanatory notes for finalization and adoption by the Commission. At the present session, the Commission had before it the draft UNCITRAL model clauses on specialized express dispute resolution (A/CN.9/1181), as well as the reports of Working Group II on the work of its seventy-eighth session (A/CN.9/1159) and seventy-ninth session (A/CN.9/1166).

B. Consideration of the draft model clauses and the explanatory notes

81. The Commission considered the text of the draft model clauses and the explanatory notes as follows.

82. With regard to the model clause on highly expedited arbitration, a proposal to amend the chapeau to include the terms "formation", "applicability" and "enforceability" and to replace the term "invalidity" with "validity" did not receive support.

83. Concerns were raised about the fourth sentence of paragraph 18 of the explanatory notes, which indicated that courts might refuse to set aside a non-reasoned award because they could not assess the underlying grounds. It was recommended that the statement be clarified by providing further context and explanation.

84. With regard to the model clause on adjudication, there was a proposal to delete option II of paragraph 2 and include it in the explanatory notes for the following reasons: (a) adjudication was a simplified method of resolving a dispute that could always be followed by full arbitration proceedings if a party was dissatisfied with the adjudicated result, such that limiting adjudication to only certain types of disputes while arbitration could cover all disputes created an unnecessarily fragmented

[15] Ibid., *Seventy-seventh Session, Supplement No. 17* (A/77/17), paras. 223–225.

procedure; (b) the wording of that option was unclear, consisted of heterogeneous elements that were not carefully examined and risked creating legal uncertainty; and (c) a limitation on the scope of adjudication would likely give rise to frequent disagreements as to whether a given matter fell clearly or wholly within the jurisdictional limitation, in circumstances where the adjudicator had insufficient time to address both jurisdiction and the merits and where the adjudicator's competence to rule on his or her own jurisdiction might also be contested. Moreover, as the adjudicator could decide that a dispute was not suitable for adjudication in accordance with subparagraph (g), it would be superfluous to suggest a limitation on scope.

85. In response, it was noted that: (a) option II was a compromise to address concerns about an overly broad scope for adjudication, as the option might not be suitable or could be detrimental to the usability of the model clause on adjudication in jurisdictions where users might be concerned with adjudication that was not limited to monetary claims or claims related to other particular aspects of contracts; (b) parties should be given the flexibility to exclude certain issues, because adjudication without limitations on scope could create significant legal uncertainty given that the model clause included two arbitration mechanisms and there could be overlap between the different procedures; (c) there was a need to alert parties of that flexibility in the model clause itself and to explicitly include examples of limitations on scope in the text of the model clause, rather than just in the explanatory notes; (d) a limitation on the scope of adjudication was not novel, as evidenced by laws in some jurisdictions; and (e) reliance on the discretion of the adjudicator to decide on the suitability of a claim for adjudication would not resolve the legal uncertainty noted above.

86. After discussion, the Commission decided to retain option II and agreed that it would read as follows:

> "Any dispute relating to [certain possible disputes under the contract*] may be determined by adjudication in accordance with the following subparagraphs. Any disagreement as to whether a dispute referred to the adjudicator falls within the limited scope specified by the parties in the prior sentence shall be resolved by the adjudicator.
>
> "* For example, claims solely for monetary relief."

87. A suggestion to further clarify the link between adjudication in paragraph 2 and compliance arbitration in paragraph 3 of the model clause did not receive support.

88. Concerns were raised about the text following paragraph 5, specifically the note in italics and the optional addition to paragraph 5. After deliberation, it was agreed to keep the model clause concise and to relocate the note in italics to the explanatory notes.

89. Proposals to change the name of the model clauses to make it more suitable and ensure a pertinent abbreviation in relation to the six official United Nations languages did not receive support.

Conclusion and the way forward

90. The Commission adopted the UNCITRAL Model Clauses on Specialized Express Dispute Resolution, subject to the above-mentioned changes.

91. With regard to the guidance text on evidence, a suggestion was made to include it in the explanatory notes given its value as an outcome of the negotiations. However, that suggestion did not receive support, as the current guidance was too generic to be effective. As a result of the discussion, the Commission decided not to attach the guidance text on evidence to the model clauses, but to consider developing it further as part of the ongoing stocktaking project on dispute resolution in the digital economy.

92. Given the limited time available, the Commission agreed to task Working Group II with finalizing the text of the explanatory notes at its eightieth session, in 2024.

C. Adoption of the UNCITRAL Model Clauses on Specialized Express Dispute Resolution

93. After completing its consideration of the draft model clauses on specialized express dispute resolution with accompanying explanatory notes (A/CN.9/1181), the Commission adopted by consensus the following decision at its 1217th meeting, on 1 July 2024:

"*The United Nations Commission on International Trade Law*,

"*Recalling* its mandate under General Assembly resolution 2205 (XXI) of 17 December 1966 to further the progressive harmonization and unification of the law of international trade and in that respect to bear in mind the interests of all peoples, in particular those of developing countries, in the extensive development of international trade,

"*Recalling also* its decision at the fifty-fifth session, in 2022, to entrust Working Group II (Dispute Settlement) with considering the topics of technology-related dispute resolution and adjudication jointly, and with considering ways to further accelerate the resolution of disputes,[16]

"*Recognizing* the value of model clauses on specialized express dispute resolution, which provide parties with a streamlined and simplified procedure for settling disputes that arise in the context of international commercial relations within a shortened time frame,

"*Recognizing also* the need to balance the efficiency of arbitral proceedings with the rights of disputing parties to due process and fair treatment,

"*Noting* that the preparation of the draft model clauses on specialized express dispute resolution and the explanatory notes benefited greatly from consultations with Governments and interested intergovernmental and international non-governmental organizations,

"*Expressing* its appreciation to Working Group II for its work in developing the draft model clauses on specialized express dispute resolution and the explanatory notes and to relevant international intergovernmental and non-governmental organizations for their support and contributions,

"1. *Adopts* the UNCITRAL Model Clauses on Specialized Express Dispute Resolution, as contained in annex II to the report of the United Nations Commission on International Trade Law on the work of its fifty-seventh session;[17]

"2. *Approves* in principle the draft explanatory notes to the UNCITRAL Model Clauses on Specialized Express Dispute Resolution contained in document A/CN.9/1181, as revised by the Commission at its fifty-seventh session, and authorizes Working Group II (Dispute Settlement) to edit and finalize the text at its eightieth session, in 2024;

"3. *Recommends* the use of the UNCITRAL Model Clauses on Specialized Express Dispute Resolution by parties and administering institutions in the settlement of disputes arising in the context of international commercial relations;

"4. *Requests* the Secretary-General to publish the UNCITRAL Model Clauses on Specialized Express Dispute Resolution and the final text of the explanatory notes, including electronically, in the six official languages of the United Nations, and to make all efforts to ensure that they become generally known and available."

[16] Ibid.

[17] Ibid., *Seventy-ninth Session, Supplement No. 17* (A/79/17), annex II.

VI. Consideration of texts prepared in the context of investor-State dispute settlement reform

A. Introduction

94. The Commission recalled that, at its fiftieth session, in 2017, it had entrusted Working Group III with a broad mandate to work on the possible reform of investor-State dispute settlement.[18] The Commission also recalled that, at its fifty-sixth session, in 2023, it had expressed its satisfaction with the progress made by the Working Group and encouraged it to submit the draft provisions on an advisory centre on international investment law and a guidance text on means to prevent and mitigate disputes for consideration by the Commission at the present session.[19]

95. The Commission noted that Working Group III had conducted work on the draft statute of an advisory centre on international investment dispute resolution during its forty-third, forty-sixth, forty-seventh and forty-eighth sessions, the text of which was approved by the Working Group at its forty-eighth session, in April 2024 (A/CN.9/1184, paras. 1 and 2).

96. The Commission further noted that Working Group III had considered the draft toolkit on prevention and mitigation of international investment disputes during its forty-fifth, forty-seventh and forty-eighth sessions, the text of which was submitted to the Commission for it to take note of the progress made so far and to provide further guidance as necessary (A/CN.9/1167, para. 83).

97. At the present session, the Commission had before it the following documents: (a) the draft statute of an advisory centre on international investment dispute resolution (A/CN.9/1184); and (b) the draft toolkit on prevention and mitigation of international investment disputes (A/CN.9/1185).

B. Finalization and adoption in principle of the Statute of the Advisory Centre on International Investment Dispute Resolution

1. Consideration of the draft statute of an advisory centre on international investment dispute resolution (A/CN.9/1184)

Article 1. Establishment

98. The Commission approved article 1 unchanged.

Article 2. Objectives

99. With regard to article 2, proposals to combine the two paragraphs into a single paragraph and to use either the word "support" or "assistance" did not receive support.

100. The Commission approved article 2 unchanged.

Article 3. General principles

101. With regard to paragraph 1, a proposal to include "transparency" as an additional general principle did not receive support, given that the operation of the Advisory Centre might require confidentiality, particularly in providing the services referred to in article 7. In that regard, it was pointed out that the governance structure set out in article 5 could be revised to ensure appropriate transparency in the administration of the Centre, particularly with regard to its financial operations (see para. 108 below).

102. With regard to paragraph 3, it was agreed that the phrase "as appropriate" should be placed before the word "cooperate" to ensure that the phrase qualified both the

[18] Ibid., *Seventy-second Session, Supplement No. 17* (A/72/17), para. 264.
[19] Ibid., *Seventy-eighth Session, Supplement No. 17* (A/78/17), paras. 151 and 152.

words "cooperate" and "coordinate". Subject to that change, the Commission approved article 3.

Article 4. Membership

103. With regard to the participation of regional economic integration organizations, it was suggested that the draft statute should address additional aspects, such as how a regional economic integration organization could become a Member of the Centre, conditions thereto and voting rules in relation to members of the regional economic integration organization. In response, it was suggested that those issues would be better addressed in the multilateral instrument on investor-State dispute settlement reform, which could provide a default rule for the different protocols of that instrument. A proposal to include references to the multilateral instrument on investor-State dispute settlement reform in the draft statute itself did not receive support. The Commission was reminded that no final decision had been made as to whether the draft statute would be included as a protocol to the multilateral instrument or presented as a separate instrument. In that connection, it was noted that Working Group III was expected to begin considering the multilateral instrument at its forty-ninth session.

104. After discussion, the Commission confirmed that the draft statute, in particular article 4, paragraph 1, reflected its understanding that a regional economic integration organization could be a Member of the Advisory Centre with its own rights and obligations, including the right to vote and the obligation to pay financial contributions. It was further confirmed that member States of a regional economic integration organization could not vote or benefit from the services of the Centre unless they were Members themselves, and vice versa. In view of the fact that the Commission was expected to adopt the statute in principle (which meant that it might be subject to further adjustments, as necessary), it was agreed that the participation of regional economic integration organizations would need further consideration in the context of the multilateral instrument on investor-State dispute settlement reform (including whether they would count as a Party in addition to their member States, as well as the voting rules).

105. Given that the categorization of Members in annexes was subject to further consideration, it was agreed that the phrase "annex I, annex II or annex III" in paragraph 3 would be placed in square brackets.

Article 5. Structure

106. A proposal to include a provision addressing disputes among Members and conflicts arising from the operation of the Advisory Centre (including among staff members of the Secretariat of the Centre) did not receive support, in light of article 5, which addressed the governance structure of the Centre and contained rules on accountability and decision-making. It was further stated that including such a provision might lead to complexities and harm the effective operation of the Centre, and that the relevant aspects could be addressed in the rules of procedure to be adopted by the Governing Committee.

107. It was agreed to remove the square brackets around the phrase "and those of the Executive Committee" in paragraph 3 (a) and around the phrase "prepared by the Executive Director" in paragraph 6 (c).

108. With regard to paragraph 3 (a), (b), (e), (g) and (h), it was agreed to add the words "and publish" after the word "adopt" with the aim of enhancing the transparency of the Centre's operations.

109. It was agreed to place the phrase "annexes I, II and III" in the third sentence of paragraph 5 in square brackets (see para. 105 above). Similarly, it was agreed to put the words "six" in the first sentence and "two" in the third sentence in square brackets, as the number of annexes categorizing the Members would determine the appropriate numbers to be included.

110. With regard to paragraphs 7 to 9, it was understood that the rules on decision-making would be further detailed in the rules of procedure to be adopted by the Governing Committee (for example, the meaning of "consensus" and "presence" and that the quorum required for the "first vote" would not apply to the "second vote").

111. It was agreed that the heading for paragraphs 10 to 12 should include the words "and the Secretariat".

112. Subject to the above-mentioned changes (paras. 107–109 and 111), the Commission approved article 5.

Article 6. Technical assistance and capacity-building

113. It was clarified that paragraph 1 (e) did not refer to the Centre functioning as a depositary of funds (financial resources) relating to proceedings, but rather as a repository of resources relating to information about international investment dispute resolution.

114. It was agreed that paragraph 2 could be deleted, as it was already addressed by article 3, paragraph 3. Subject to that change, the Commission approved article 6.

Article 7. Legal advice and support with regard to international investment dispute proceedings

115. A suggestion to include a paragraph similar to article 6, paragraph 3, in article 7 indicating that the Centre could engage other persons or entities in providing legal advice and support did not receive support.

116. It was agreed that the words "a team of" in paragraph 1 (d) should be deleted and that the words "annex II" in paragraph 3 should be placed in square brackets. Subject to those changes, the Commission approved article 7.

Article 8. Financing

117. It was agreed that references to annexes I, II, III and IV in paragraphs 2 and 3 should be placed in square brackets pending further consideration of the categorization of Members. Subject to that change, the Commission approved article 8.

Article 9. Legal status and liability

118. It was widely felt that there would be merit in establishing the Centre within the United Nations system. It was also widely felt that the establishment and operation of the Centre should not have any implications for the regular budget of the United Nations.

119. In that context, the Commission was informed about possible ways to establish the Centre within the United Nations system, particularly as a subsidiary organ of the General Assembly, a specialized agency or a related organization. It was observed that depending on how the Centre was established within the United Nations system (including any relationship agreement to be concluded with the United Nations), some of the articles in the draft statute might need to be adjusted.

120. In that regard, a number of questions were raised, including: (a) whether the membership features of the Centre (in particular, the mandatory financial contribution requirement or the fact that Members of the Centre might not be the same as members of the United Nations) would pose challenges in establishing the Centre as a subsidiary organ of the General Assembly; (b) how privileges and immunities granted to the Centre and its staff members would differ; (c) whether and how participation of non-Members as observers of the Centre might be affected; (d) whether an organization that met the criteria under Articles 57 and 63 of the Charter of the United Nations must be established as a specialized agency; (e) whether the statute becoming a protocol to a United Nations convention would have an impact on the status of the Centre; (f) whether a subsidiary organ of the General Assembly could be funded entirely by

extrabudgetary resources; (g) whether the Secretariat of the United Nations could function as an interim or permanent secretariat of the Centre and if so, whether that could be done without any implications for the regular budget of the United Nations; and (h) aspects to be addressed in a relationship agreement and how and when it would be negotiated and concluded. It was suggested that those issues could be addressed as part of the Centre's operationalization.

121. With regard to paragraph 1, it was agreed that the paragraph should be split into two sentences, as the capacity referred to in the second part did not relate to "international legal personality". Accordingly, it was agreed that paragraph 1 should read as follows: "The Advisory Centre shall have full international legal personality. The legal capacity of the Advisory Centre shall include the capacity to contract, to acquire and dispose of immovable and movable property and to institute legal proceedings."

122. With regard to paragraph 2, doubts were expressed about the need for the second sentence. In response, it was mentioned that the sentence provided for a mechanism for relocating the headquarters in limited circumstances, mainly to ensure the Centre's operational effectiveness. It was clarified that the Governing Committee would be able to take such a decision in accordance with article 5, paragraphs 7 and 8, and that in the case of a temporary relocation, the Governing Committee could establish when or under what conditions the headquarters would return to its original location. Lastly, it was confirmed that an amendment to the first sentence of paragraph 2 to reflect the new permanent location based on a decision taken by the Governing Committee would be subject to the process outlined in article 15, paragraphs 1 and 2, addressing amendments to articles of the statute.

123. The Commission agreed that the location of the headquarters of the Centre should be set forth in the statute. It was anticipated that the Commission would indicate the location of the headquarters when it presented the statute as a protocol to the multilateral instrument on investor-State dispute settlement reform to the General Assembly.

124. A suggestion was made to split the first sentence of paragraph 2, as the location of the headquarters would not be "based" on the host country agreement. Accordingly, it was agreed that the sentences would read as follows: "The Advisory Centre shall be headquartered in [*to be determined*]. The Advisory Centre shall conclude a host country agreement with [*host State/Government to be determined*]."

125. A wide range of views were expressed on the criteria for determining the location of the headquarters. One view was that the headquarters should be in a neutral location or a location where appropriate guarantees were provided, which would, inter alia, allow the Centre to operate without being restricted by sanctions, including in the provision of services to its Members, with regard to both its staff members and its financial operations. Another view was that the headquarters should be easily accessible to Members, both in the geographical and economic sense (and with regard to travel requirements), in particular to the beneficiaries. In that context, the need to consider the potential Members of the Centre was underlined. Yet another view was that the headquarters (or its regional offices) should be proximate to major places of arbitration, dispute resolution institutions, hearing facilities and other venues, where the Centre would be providing services. The view was also expressed that the Centre should be headquartered in a developing country, which could promote equitable geographical distribution of international organizations and services and align with the broader agenda of the Sustainable Development Goals by fostering inclusiveness, reducing global inequalities and promoting stronger international institutions. It was noted that the location should ensure the effective and sustainable operation of the Centre, including by attracting qualified staff members and providing robust infrastructure. It was further noted that the host Government's willingness to support and contribute to the sustainable operation of the Centre should be taken into account. It was generally felt that all such factors should be considered holistically, especially

with a view to establishing the headquarters and one or more regional offices, without any one of the factors unduly limiting a State from hosting the Centre.

126. The Governments of Armenia, Côte d'Ivoire, the Democratic Republic of the Congo, France, Ghana, Paraguay and Thailand expressed their interest in hosting the headquarters of the Advisory Centre or regional offices thereof. The Commission expressed its gratitude to those Governments for their interest. Noting that the time frame for expressing interest had not expired, the Commission also called on other States to express their interest.

127. With regard to paragraph 4, a proposal to replace the phrase "as set out in this Protocol" with "necessary for the independent exercise of its functions in accordance with this Protocol" did not receive support.

128. In order to address issues relating to documents received and produced by the Centre in providing its services, it was agreed that the following paragraph would be inserted after paragraph 4: "The archives of the Advisory Centre shall be inviolable, wherever they may be."

129. With regard to the phrase "when the Advisory Centre waives this immunity" in paragraphs 5 and 7, it was understood that the rules of procedure to be adopted by the Governing Committee would establish the process for waiving immunity, including the authority to take such decisions.

130. A suggestion that paragraph 6 should be the subject of further consideration as a matter of operationalization did not receive support.

131. Given that paragraph 7 provided for functional immunity regardless of the nationality of staff members, it was questioned whether it would be possible for a Member to limit the immunity provided therein to a staff member of its nationality. In response, it was noted that it would be left to the Advisory Centre to determine whether and under what circumstances it would waive the immunity of a staff member.

132. It was agreed that paragraph 8 should be simplified to read: "No tax shall be levied on or in respect of salaries, expense allowances or other emoluments paid by the Advisory Centre to the Executive Director and the staff members of the Secretariat".

133. Subject to the above-mentioned changes, the Commission approved article 9.

Article 10. Reservations

134. The Commission approved article 10 unchanged.

Article 11. Depositary and Article 12. Signature, ratification, acceptance, approval, accession

135. It was observed that articles 11 and 12 might not be necessary if the multilateral instrument on investor-State dispute settlement reform, to which the statute was expected to form a protocol, sufficiently addressed the depositary and means of becoming a Party to the statute.

136. It was suggested that the statute should include an additional article detailing the participation of regional economic integration organizations. Reference was made to article 12 of the United Nations Convention on International Settlement Agreements resulting from Mediation (the Singapore Convention on Mediation),[20] which addressed issues of competence and the declaration to be made by a regional economic integration organization when depositing its instrument.

137. In response, it was recalled that the Commission had agreed to address the issues arising from the participation of regional economic integration organizations in the context of the multilateral instrument on investor-State dispute settlement reform and

[20] Ibid., *Seventy-third Session, Supplement No. 17* (A/73/17), annex I.

not necessarily in the statute (see para. 104). Reference was also made to article 8 of the United Nations Convention on Transparency in Treaty-based Investor-State Arbitration (the Mauritius Convention),[21] which did not contain detailed provisions on the participation of regional economic integration organizations. A question was raised about the competence that would be required of a regional economic integration organization to become a Member of the Centre, as the key obligation under the statute would be to contribute to its budget. In light of the fact that regional economic integration organizations could potentially become donors, it was stated that imposing stringent requirements on their participation could have a negative impact on the overall operation of the Centre.

138. After discussion, the Commission approved articles 11 and 12 unchanged.

Article 13. Entry into force

139. With regard to paragraph 1, diverging views were expressed about whether the condition that the expected contributions must exceed a certain amount should be included as a factor for determining the entry into force of the statute. It was explained that the inclusion of such a condition would ensure an adequate level of resources for the Centre to begin its operations. However, questions were raised about how that determination would be made and by whom (given that the governance structure of the Centre could not be operational until the entry into force of the statute) and how the expected contributions of Members would be calculated (given the various methods for making payments). Therefore, a suggestion was made to remove that condition and leave the decision to the Governing Committee. It was also suggested that the drafting could be improved in order to clarify the timing of when the statute would enter into force.

140. After discussion, the Commission agreed to revise paragraph 1 as follows:

> "1. This Protocol shall enter into force six months following the date upon which the following conditions are met:
>
> (a) [*Number to be determined, including the possibility of requiring a certain number from each group of Members*] instruments of ratification, acceptance, approval or accession have been deposited; and
>
> (b) The total amount of contributions that States or regional economic integration organizations that are Parties to the Protocol are obliged to make in accordance with [annex IV] exceeds [*an amount to be determined*]."

141. It was agreed that the number and the amount in subparagraphs (a) and (b) should be considered during the operationalization process.

142. With regard to paragraph 2, a suggestion to require a State to pay its contributions for the statute to enter into force for that State did not receive support. It was generally felt that the 30-day period in paragraph 2 appropriately addressed the possible urgent need of States to benefit from the services of the Centre soon after depositing their instrument of accession.

143. Subject to the above-mentioned change (see para. 140 above), the Commission approved article 13.

Article 14. Annexes

144. The Commission approved article 14 unchanged.

---

[21] United Nations, *Treaty Series*, vol. 3208.

Article 15. Amendments to the Protocol and annexes

145. Given that the Commission had not fixed the number of annexes in which to categorize potential Members, it was agreed that the numbering of the annexes in the statute should be placed in square brackets.

146. With regard to paragraph 4, it was agreed that a comma should be placed before the word "only" in the chapeau, which would clarify that the paragraph aimed to limit the situations in which the Governing Committee could adopt amendments to the annexes. With regard to subparagraph (a), it was agreed that the words "any changes to" should be retained outside square brackets. It was observed that subparagraphs (b) to (d) would need to be adjusted depending on the annexes to be developed and the objective criteria to classify the Members.

147. Subject to those changes, the Commission approved article 15.

Article 16. Withdrawal and termination

148. The Commission approved article 16 unchanged.

Annexes I to III

149. It was generally felt that there would be merit in categorizing States and regional economic integration organizations in the statute for the purposes of determining the priority to be given to a certain group of States in obtaining the services of the centre and the minimum contributions to be made by the different groups of States.

150. The view was expressed that the list in the annexes should only include Members of the Advisory Centre and not all States Members of the United Nations. However, the Commission confirmed that when finalizing the statute, States Members of the United Nations should be listed in the different annexes, which would clarify the category into which a State would be placed when it became a Member of the Centre. That would be important as it would allow States to assess their rights and obligations under the statute.

151. It was widely felt that the categorization should be based on objective criteria. As for annex I, it was agreed that the list of least developed countries adopted by the General Assembly should form the basis. With regard to the other annexes, the following were mentioned as possible objective criteria:

(a) The needs of States to access the services of the Centre (including whether they lacked or had the human and financial resources to prevent and handle disputes and to seek external counsel);

(b) The capacity of States to make the necessary financial contributions to support the Centre, as well as their willingness to possibly forego some of the services or priority provided under the statute;

(c) Development indicators (such as gross domestic product per capita);

(d) The role of States in the global economy (such as trade volume, gross domestic product and investment flows);

(e) The extent of the involvement of States in international investment disputes.

152. It was suggested that criteria used by other international organizations to categorize States could be examined and presented for consideration as part of the Centre's operationalization. In that regard, it was mentioned that the reliability of such criteria should be assessed, as the context in which they were taken into account might differ and the criteria to be developed should address the needs of the statute and be geared towards the investor-State dispute settlement context.

153. It was also suggested that States should be given the opportunity to express their views on their categorization and that such views should be taken into consideration, although that would not necessarily amount to a State being able to declare which

category it should be placed in (unless it opted to make a greater contribution to the budget as a donor in the context of article 15, paragraph 4).

154. It was further suggested that reference could be made to scales of contributions by States in other international organizations, including the United Nations, which could obviate the need to develop separate criteria or the need for categorization entirely, as a similar formula could be followed.

155. After discussion, the Commission agreed that the annexes to the statute would be formulated as follows and that the lists of States would be finalized when the statute was eventually submitted for adoption by the General Assembly:

"*Annex I*

[*This Annex would reflect the list of least developed countries adopted by the United Nations General Assembly when the statute is finalized.*]

"*Annexes [II and III]*

[*Annexes [II and III] would list the States Members of the United Nations not listed in annex I. Those States would be categorized in accordance with the objective criteria to be developed for that purpose. The lists would also include regional economic integration organizations*.]"

Annex on the scale of minimum contributions

156. The Commission confirmed that the scale of minimum contributions by Members to be listed in the annexes should be sliding, with that of Members listed in annex I being the lowest. It was further confirmed that there could be different types of contributions (for example, annual, multi-year and one-time contributions).

Operationalization of the Advisory Centre

157. It was widely felt that the operationalization of the Advisory Centre would require further preparatory work.

158. The Commission agreed that the basis of the preparatory work should be the statute as adopted in principle by the Commission (see annex III of the present report). It was further agreed that the preparatory work should address issues such as: (a) ways to establish the Advisory Centre within the United Nations system based entirely on extrabudgetary resources; (b) criteria for determining the location of the headquarters and regional offices; (c) the anticipated budget based on potential membership and workload, and the need to ensure sustainable operations; (d) the amount of contributions by Members and methods of payment; (e) objective criteria for classifying States in the annexes; (f) thresholds of membership and contributions for the entry into force of the statute; and (g) decisions, rules and regulations to be adopted by the Governing Committee, including staff and financial regulations. As an indicative list of issues to be tackled, it was agreed that priority might be given to certain issues as progress was made in the preparatory work (see para. 162 below).

159. The Commission agreed that in order to facilitate the preparatory work, it would utilize an informal process involving all States and regional economic integration organizations. It was agreed that as an informal process, no decisions should be made, and efforts should be made to maintain the transparency and inclusiveness of the process by ensuring remote participation and by making a summary of the informal discussions available. It was further agreed that the informal process should be led by the bureau of the Commission and the bureau of Working Group III.

160. Views diverged on whether the informal process should be reported back on directly to the Commission or through Working Group III. One view was that deliberations within the Working Group could allow an in-depth discussion, ensure a more transparent and inclusive process and enable the Commission to make a more informed decision. Another view was that as the Working Group had completed its work on the Centre and the statute had been adopted in principle, the informal process

should be reported back on directly to the Commission. In support of that view, it was noted that the Working Group was expected to present a number of reform elements to the Commission the following year (see para. 246 below) and it would, therefore, not be an effective use of the limited conference resources available to the Working Group.

161. Noting that the Government of Thailand had expressed an interest in hosting a meeting on the operationalization of the Advisory Centre, the Commission decided to hold an informal meeting in Bangkok from 2 to 4 December 2024. The Commission expressed its appreciation to the Government of Thailand for its offer to host that meeting.

162. In that regard, it was agreed that the meeting in Bangkok should focus on matters pertaining to issues (a), (b) and (e) listed in paragraph 158 above and, time permitting, on those relating to issues (c), (d) and (f) in the same paragraph. It was noted that the latter set of issues were closely linked with the potential membership of the Advisory Centre and could vary depending on the discussions held in relation to the former set of issues.

163. In view of the conference resources available to the Commission for the first half of 2025, it was agreed that the results of the meeting in Bangkok should be reported to Working Group III at its fifty-first session. The Commission agreed that that session, to be held in New York, would be composed of two parts. The first part would be held for two days during the week of 17 to 21 February 2025 and the second part would be held from 7 to 11 April 2025 (see para. 375 below). The summary of the meeting in Bangkok would be presented during the first part of the session for discussion and the exchange of views, without the Working Group needing to take any decisions on the summary. The secretariat was requested to facilitate full online participation for the first part of the session. It was agreed that the Working Group could make use of the conference time to advance other reform elements during the first part. It was further agreed that a summary of the informal meeting in Bangkok and of the discussions held during the Working Group session on the operationalization of the Advisory Centre should be presented to the Commission at its session next year.

164. The secretariat was requested to provide support for the preparatory work and the informal process, including the preparation of informal documents and the provision of partial travel support to participants from developing countries, subject to available resources. It was agreed that such support should not be to the detriment of the provision by the secretariat of services to the other working groups and the Commission overall.

165. The secretariat was further requested to organize additional informal meetings, including in a virtual format and on the margins of the Working Group III sessions to be held in 2024 and 2025, if necessary. The secretariat was also asked to consult with Governments that had expressed an interest in hosting additional informal meetings on the operationalization of the Centre (Armenia, France and others).

166. Lastly, given the concerns expressed about the informality of the process and the exceptional circumstances under which the Commission was taking the above-mentioned decisions, it was agreed that those decisions should not set a precedent for the Commission, in particular concerning the development of other investor-State dispute settlement reform elements.

2. Adoption in principle of the Statue of the Advisory Centre on International Investment Dispute Resolution

167. At its 1222nd meeting, on 5 July 2024, the Commission adopted by consensus the following decision:

"*The United Nations Commission on International Trade Law*,

"*Recalling* its mandate under General Assembly resolution 2205 (XXI) of 17 December 1966 to further the progressive harmonization and unification of the law of international trade and in that respect to bear in mind the interests of all peoples, in particular those of developing countries, in the extensive development of international trade,

"*Recalling also* its decision at the fiftieth session, in July 2017, to entrust Working Group III (Investor-State Dispute Settlement Reform) with a broad mandate to work on the possible reform of investor-State dispute settlement and to develop relevant solutions,[22]

"*Noting* that in carrying out its mandate, the Working Group had identified the desirability of establishing an advisory centre to address the urgent need to provide training, support and assistance with regard to international investment dispute resolution, in particular to least developed and developing countries, which could enhance the legitimacy of the international investment dispute resolution system more broadly,

"*Recognizing* that the establishment of an advisory centre could enhance the capacity of States and regional economic integration organizations to prevent and handle international investment disputes, in particular least developed countries and developing countries,

"*Recognizing also* that the services envisaged by the advisory centre, including technical assistance and capacity-building activities, as well as legal advice and support with regard to international investment dispute proceedings, would benefit relevant stakeholders involved in international investment dispute resolution,

"*Recognizing further* that the establishment of an advisory centre would require a statute setting forth rules on its creation, objectives, general principles, membership, structure, services to be provided and other related issues,

"*Acknowledging* that the establishment and operationalization of the advisory centre would need further preparatory work involving States and regional economic integration organizations interested in the advisory centre and that such a process should be conducted in a transparent and inclusive manner,

"*Mindful* that the Working Group is continuing to make progress with regard to a number of investor-State dispute settlement reform elements to be recommended to the Commission,

"*Mindful also* that the Working Group is considering the development of a multilateral instrument to implement those reform elements and that the statute of the advisory centre could form one of the protocols to such an instrument,

"*Noting* that the preparation of the draft statute of the advisory centre benefited greatly from consultations with Governments and interested intergovernmental and non-governmental organizations,

"*Expressing* its appreciation to Working Group III for formulating the draft statute of the advisory centre on international investment dispute resolution,

"1. *Adopts* in principle the Statute of the Advisory Centre on International Investment Dispute Resolution, as contained in annex III to the report of the United Nations Commission on International Trade Law on the work of its fifty-seventh session;[23]

"2. *Recommends* that all States and regional economic integration organizations take part in the preparatory work to operationalize the Advisory Centre on International Investment Dispute Resolution;

"3. *Requests* the Secretary-General to publish the Statute, including electronically, in the six official languages of the United Nations."

---

[22] *Official Records of the General Assembly, Seventy-second Session, Supplement No. 17* (A/72/17), para. 264.

[23] Ibid., *Seventy-ninth Session, Supplement No. 17* (A/79/17), annex III.

C. Consideration of the draft toolkit on prevention and mitigation of international investment disputes

168. The Commission noted the current status of work on the draft toolkit on prevention and mitigation of international investment disputes (A/CN.9/1185). At the outset, the importance of dispute prevention and mitigation was acknowledged, and it was widely felt that the toolkit should continue to be developed as a descriptive document illustrating how States had set up and implemented dispute prevention and mitigation systems. In that context, it was mentioned that there was merit in maintaining the toolkit as an evolving document to reflect States' existing and new practices.

169. In terms of how best to advance the work, the secretariat was requested to circulate the draft toolkit for comments and feedback by States, on the basis of which an updated version of the toolkit could be prepared. The secretariat was further requested to report on the progress made and inform the Commission when the toolkit was ready for finalization. The Commission called on all States and organizations to share information on existing practices for inclusion in the draft toolkit and to verify the correctness of the information contained therein.

VII. Consideration of the draft provisions on automated contracting and guide to enactment

A. Introduction

170. The Commission recalled that, at its fifty-fifth session, in 2022, it had requested Working Group IV to deal with the topic of automated contracting in the following two stages: (a) as a first stage, to compile provisions of UNCITRAL texts that applied to automated contracting and revise those provisions, as appropriate; and (b) as a second stage, to identify and develop possible new provisions that addressed a broader range of issues.[24] The Commission had before it the draft provisions on automated contracting (A/CN.9/1178), which reflected the outcome of the work carried out by the Working Group, as well as the accompanying draft guide to enactment (A/CN.9/1179).

B. Consideration of the draft provisions and guide to enactment

Article 1. Definitions

171. The Commission heard several proposals to amend the definition of "automated system" in paragraph 1 (a) to align it more closely with terminology in the United Nations Convention on the Use of Electronic Communications in International Contracts (the Electronic Communications Convention).

172. Firstly, a proposal was made to define automated systems as "computer programs" rather than as "computer systems", given that the latter term was not defined in the draft provisions or in other UNCITRAL texts. In response, it was noted that the broader concept of "computer system" was more accurate and was sufficiently circumscribed in paragraph 23 of the draft guide to enactment.

173. Secondly, a proposal was made to remove the word "necessary", which could inadvertently exclude systems for which human oversight was required under other law. In response, it was observed that the word "necessary" had been inserted purposefully by the Working Group to ensure that such systems were covered, and that the explanation in paragraph 25 of the draft guide to enactment was sufficient to avoid any doubt.

[24] Ibid., *Seventy-seventh Session, Supplement No. 17* (A/77/17), para. 159.

174. Thirdly, it was observed that the word "actions" in the English language version was not used in all language versions consistently with how it was used in article 4 (g) of the Electronic Communications Convention; it was agreed that linguistic consistency with that Convention should be maintained.

175. After discussion, the Commission agreed to retain the definition of "automated system" to mean "a computer system that is capable of carrying out actions without the necessary review or intervention of a natural person".

176. It was suggested that the definition of "automated system" could be complemented by referring to use cases of automated systems in the guide to enactment. To that end, a suggestion was made to include a sentence in paragraph 26 of the draft guide along the following lines: "Examples of use cases in automated contracting include supply chain management, programmatic advertising, virtual assistants and automated pricing in electronic commerce, as well as sector-specific examples such as renewable energy trading and foreign exchange trading."

177. It was observed that use cases of automated systems were referred to elsewhere in the draft guide to enactment; the UNCITRAL secretariat was invited to review the various references to ensure congruency.

178. Given that automated contracting covered the use of artificial intelligence in the formation and performance of contracts, the Commission heard that automation should not be equated merely with the absence of human involvement, but also with the absence of predictability. The UNCITRAL secretariat was invited to review the draft guide to enactment to ensure that it clearly reflected that basic assumption.

179. The Commission heard that greater clarity was needed as to the interaction between "data messages" and "actions" carried out by an automated system. To that end, it was proposed to insert the following text at the end of the definition of "data message" in paragraph 1 (b): ", which may constitute actions in connection with the conclusion or performance of the contract or other communications". It was explained that the additional wording also provided conceptual clarity regarding the interaction between article 2, paragraph 1, and article 4. Alternatively, it was suggested to remove all references to "data message", as the term was seldom used.

180. In response, it was noted that the proposed additional wording could have the undesirable effect of limiting the scope of the term "data message" and could upset the uniform interpretation of a widely used definition. It was observed that the clarification sought was already provided in paragraph 28 of the draft guide to enactment. After discussion, the Commission agreed to retain the definition of "data message" without amendment.

181. Turning to paragraph 2, the Commission agreed not to retain the words in square brackets, which could introduce doubt as to the scope of the definition of "automated system" in paragraph 1. A suggestion was made to incorporate the substance of the remainder of paragraph 2 into the definition of "automated system". The Commission agreed to consider the suggestion at a later stage, if need be.

Article 2. Scope of application

182. The need to clarify that the draft provisions applied to all stages of the contract life cycle was emphasized. Broad support was expressed for that view. It was stressed that article 2 should expressly refer to the pre-contractual stage and to contract termination, in addition to contract formation and performance. It was added that the contract life cycle encompassed the exercise of agreed remedies. Suggestions were made to modify article 2 to reflect those understandings, including by inserting in paragraph 1 (a) a reference to the information given prior to the conclusion of a contract.

183. In response, it was noted that the references to "formation" and "performance" of the contract, which were usual in UNCITRAL texts, were understood as covering all stages of the contract life cycle. The desirability of keeping the text in line with existing UNCITRAL texts was stressed, including with a view to the expected future

interaction of the draft provisions with those texts. At the same time, it was acknowledged that there was scope to elaborate on the scope of those concepts in paragraphs 1 (a) and 1 (b).

184. It was emphasized that automated systems could operate in any or all of the various stages of the contract life cycle. It was suggested that the word "and" in the chapeau of paragraph 1 should be replaced with "or" to reflect that (see also A/CN.9/1162, para. 14) and that the guide to enactment should be amended to convey that understanding. The Commission agreed with that suggestion.

185. It was indicated that the pre-contractual stage had different meanings in different jurisdictions and that reference to it should therefore be avoided, including in the guide to enactment (A/CN.9/1179, para. 30). In response, it was stressed that such reference was essential. One suggestion was to delete the word "pre-contractual" and to refer instead to negotiations or preliminary dealings.

186. In view of the fact that the operation of an automated system did not necessarily coincide with its use, broad support was expressed for adding a reference to "use" in paragraph 2.

187. In relation to the earlier discussion (see para. 179 above), the view was reiterated that the definition of "data message" was unnecessary, and that article 2 should instead define the concept of "action" along the lines of paragraph 24 of the draft guide to enactment. It was explained that automated systems produced output in the form of data messages and actions. It was also explained that a data message could initiate a change in status of hardware, such as the opening or closing of a pipe.

188. After discussion, the Commission agreed to: (a) insert at the end of paragraph 1 (b) the words ", such as its modification or termination"; (b) further clarify the relationship between the notions of "data message" and "action" in the guide to enactment; and (c) replace the words "or operation" with the words "operation or use" in paragraph 2.

189. It was suggested that the reference to high-frequency trading in paragraph 32 of the draft guide to enactment should be amended to clarify that such trading was a type of algorithmic trading. Another suggestion was to further explain in the remarks on paragraph 2 that the draft provisions did not affect the application of mandatory law (A/CN.9/1179, para. 33).

Article 3. Technology neutrality

190. It was recalled that article 3 applied throughout the contract life cycle and that that should be reiterated in the remarks on article 3 in the draft guide to enactment.

191. A question was asked about the use of the word "method". It was recalled that "method" was a term commonly used in UNCITRAL texts, and it was suggested that the guide to enactment should be expanded by drawing on the explanatory materials referenced in footnote 19 of the draft guide. The Commission agreed to that suggestion. In addition, it was suggested that article 3 should also refer to "technologies". In response, it was noted that the term "method" was understood to cover technologies.

192. It was also indicated that article 3 was aimed at ensuring that the draft provisions did not mandate or favour the use of any particular method, technology or product. Broad support was expressed for that goal. It was explained that, as the draft provisions did not differentiate between different types of automated systems, it would be sufficient for article 3 to refer instead to "automated systems". After discussion, the Commission agreed to replace the words "in connection with the formation or performance of contracts" with the words "in automated systems to form or perform contracts", which reproduced wording found in article 2.

193. At the same time, broad support was also expressed for clarifying that the draft provisions did not mandate the use of automated systems to form or perform contracts. Although it was noted that a rule to that effect encompassed technology neutrality and

could therefore replace article 3 entirely, it was also noted that there was value in retaining a specific rule that the provisions did not mandate the use of a particular method. It was acknowledged that a rule on voluntary use and a rule on technology neutrality could be combined in the same provision; the Commission therefore agreed to reformulate article 3 as follows: "Nothing in [this instrument] requires the use of an automated system or a particular method in automated systems to form or perform contracts."

Article 4. Legal recognition of automated contracting

194. It was noted that paragraphs 2 and 3 were similar in structure and content, the only difference being that one referred to contract formation and the other to contract performance. The Commission therefore agreed to merge the two paragraphs by deleting paragraph 3 and inserting the words "or performance" after the word "formation" in paragraph 2.

195. It was recalled that article 4 applied throughout the life cycle of the contract, and that that should be reiterated in the guide to enactment (see paras. 184 and 190). In that regard, a suggestion was made to include wording along the following lines: "The terms 'formation' and 'performance' of a contract are intended to cover the various stages of the entire contract life cycle, including negotiations in the context of concluding a contract and termination." The same considerations were said to apply to articles 5 and 6.

196. It was observed that, although paragraphs 1 and 2 of article 4 were concerned with "validity" and "enforceability", only paragraph 2 was concerned with "legal effect". It was added that contracts produced legal effects and, therefore, a reference to the "legal effect" of a contract should be inserted in paragraph 1. Although some support was expressed for that suggestion, it was noted that provisions on legal recognition in existing UNCITRAL texts, such as articles 5 and 11 of the UNCITRAL Model Law on Electronic Commerce,[25] dealt only with the legal effect of actions, not contracts. The desirability of keeping the wording in line with those texts was again stressed, with the view being expressed that the Commission should not depart from the formulation in those texts without good reason. In any event, it was noted that it was sufficient for article 4 to deal only with the validity and enforceability of contracts. After discussion, the Commission agreed not to include a reference to "legal effect" in paragraph 1.

197. It was indicated that the term "enforceability" might have different meanings in different jurisdictions, which should be acknowledged in the guide to enactment.

198. The Commission heard several proposals to expand paragraph 1 to give legal recognition to contracts for which an automated system was used for contract performance but not necessarily for contract formation. It was observed that such an expansion would be particularly relevant to "smart contracts" that automated the performance of contracts through the execution of computer code. Several drafting proposals were put forward.

199. In response, the established commercial practice of using automation to perform contracts was highlighted, and it was queried whether that practice could constitute a ground for denying the validity or enforceability of the contract. It was added that, even if that was a concern in some jurisdictions, in other jurisdictions the inclusion of an expanded provision could be problematic insofar as it might imply an issue with the legality of automated contract performance when no such issue existed. It was further added that caution should be exercised in referring to "smart contracts", as the term was commonly used to refer to programs that did not constitute a contract.

200. The Commission heard that a provision covering automated contract performance could be included in the guide to enactment or as an optional provision applying the approach taken in article 1 of the UNCITRAL Model Law on Electronic Commerce.

[25] General Assembly resolution 51/162, annex.

After discussion, the Commission agreed not to retain the words in square brackets in paragraph 1 and to: (a) insert the following provision in square brackets immediately after paragraph 1: "A contract performed using an automated system shall not be denied validity or enforceability on the sole ground that no natural person reviewed or intervened in any action carried out in connection with the performance of the contract"; and (b) include a footnote to that paragraph along the following lines: "States that wish to extend the scope of article 4 to cover contracts that are performed using an automated system may wish to enact this provision."

Article 5. Legal recognition of contracts in computer code or involving dynamic information

201. The Commission agreed to retain paragraph 1 without amendment. With reference to paragraph 42 of the draft guide to enactment, it was observed that it was not correct to say that computer code was not "accessible to natural persons", but rather that it required special expertise to be interpreted by a human.

202. The need to clarify the meaning of dynamic information for the purpose of paragraph 2 was emphasized. Broad support was expressed for a suggestion to amend paragraph 43 of the draft guide to enactment to acknowledge that data sources could be internal or external to the automated system.

203. The importance of informing the parties of the use of dynamic information, and of automated systems more generally, was stressed, given that such use could raise issues of unfair or unconscionable trade practices. It was recalled that UNCITRAL texts were enabling in nature and did not prescribe information disclosure requirements, which might be regulated by other law. It was added that, although the draft guide to enactment acknowledged such laws (A/CN.9/1179, para. 33), it was useful to recall in the guide that paragraph 2 did not prejudice the application of those laws.

204. Support was expressed for replacing the word "contain" with "incorporate" in paragraph 2 (a), which reflected the terminology used in other UNCITRAL texts. A suggestion to insert the words "generating or otherwise" before the word "processing" in paragraph 2 (b) to mirror the wording of article 2, paragraph 1, was not taken up as it was felt to be unnecessary.

205. It was observed that, although article 5, paragraph 2, was formulated in similar language to article 4, the former addressed a distinct issue that was of particular significance in automated contracting. It was noted, however, that paragraph 2 was worded so generally as to cover the use of information external to the contract by any means, including non-electronic means, and it was thus suggested that the paragraph should be revised to expressly address the use of automated systems. It was also noted that paragraph 2 did not address additional challenges of using dynamic information, such as how changes were managed or documented, and it was therefore suggested that further work was needed. In response, it was noted that paragraph 2 was to be read in conjunction with article 2, and therefore only applied in the context of automated contracting. The view was expressed that, in that context, paragraph 2 sufficiently addressed the issue. Nevertheless, the Commission agreed to amend the heading of article 5 as follows: "Legal recognition of contracts in computer code and use of dynamic information in automated contracting".

206. It was observed that, by addressing contracts and actions together, paragraph 2 dealt not only with the validity and enforceability of contracts involving dynamic information but also with their "legal effect". In connection with the Commission's earlier deliberations on article 4 (see para. 196 above), it was suggested that paragraph 2 should be restructured along the lines of article 4. It was noted that the incorporation of contractual terms was a matter of contract validity and enforceability, while the processing of dynamic information to carry out actions was more a matter of the legal effect of those actions. Accordingly, it was agreed that paragraph 2 should be restructured as follows:

"2. A contract shall not be denied validity or enforceability on the sole ground that the terms of the contract incorporate information from a data source that provides information that changes periodically or continuously.

"3. An action in connection with the formation of a contract shall not be denied legal effect, validity or enforceability on the sole ground that the action involves processing data messages containing information from a source that provides information that changes periodically or continuously."

207. In response to a query, the view was expressed that it was unnecessary to address the legal recognition of the use of dynamic information to carry out actions in connection with performance of the contract. The Commission agreed that paragraph 3 of the restructured article 5 concerned only contract formation and that that should be made clear in the guide to enactment.

Article 6. Attribution of actions carried out by automated systems

208. Broad support was expressed for the view that paragraph 1 encouraged the parties to agree on attribution, which could prevent disputes. It was suggested that the words "including by reference of the parties to conditions provided by a third party" should be inserted at the end of the paragraph to provide for a common use case. In view of the statement in the draft guide to enactment that article 6 was not concerned with allocating liability, it was suggested that the guide should also state that it was not concerned with the relationship of the user of the automated system with any third-party provider, developer or operator of the automated system.

209. It was recalled that paragraph 2 attributed the action to the person using the automated system in the absence of an agreement between the parties. To better identify that person, a suggestion was made to refer to the person "having the strongest link with a specific action" in the text and to explain the concept of strongest link in the guide to enactment. In response, the view was expressed that caution should be exercised when introducing novel legal concepts in the text and preference should be given to the use of settled terminology whenever possible.

210. It was suggested that guidance on applying paragraph 2 should be provided by inserting in the text or in the guide to enactment a non-exhaustive list of relevant factors, such as the person deploying the automated system; the degree of control over the operational parameters of the system and the specific action; the material benefit or value received from the specific action; the nature and purpose of the contract; the circumstances of the case; and the practices of the parties.

211. It was also suggested that paragraph 2 could refer to the person "on whose behalf the system is used" to better identify the person who intended to use the automated system and exercised control over it, which were the defining features of a user of an automated system. In response, it was indicated that the suggested wording could introduce uncertainty, including with regard to the law of agency. After discussion, the Commission agreed to clarify in the guide to enactment that the automated system could be used on behalf of another person.

212. Different views were expressed on the "purpose" referred to in paragraph 2. One view was that the purpose was automated contracting and that, accordingly, the paragraph should refer to "the purpose of forming or performing a contract". However, it was noted that such a reference might introduce an undesirable subjective element in attribution.

213. Another view was that the purpose was the action and that, accordingly, paragraph 2 should refer to "the purpose of carrying out that action". However, it was noted that the resulting provision was circular. It was indicated that, in any event, all relevant actions pursued the goal of automated contracting and therefore it was not necessary to review each action.

214. It was noted that, while paragraph 1 referred to parties and therefore applied after the conclusion of the contract, paragraph 2 referred to persons and also applied

when a contract had not yet been formed. It was suggested that the guide to enactment should reflect that understanding.

215. After discussion, the Commission agreed to adopt article 6 with the amendment referred to in paragraph 229 below and to insert in the guide to enactment a non-exhaustive list of factors relevant to identifying the person with the strongest link to the action, as well as a discussion of the term "purpose".

Article 7. Intention, knowledge and awareness of the parties in respect of actions of automated systems

216. It was indicated that article 7 was not normative, but rather offered guidance relevant in some, but not all, cases. It was added that the parties to a contract were unlikely to have access to information on the design, commissioning and operation of an automated system, especially when that system was operated by a third party.

217. It was indicated that additional factors, such as the information shared between and with the parties, could be relevant to the article, and that party autonomy might also play a role. Broad support was expressed for considering the list of factors in article 7 non-exhaustive. It was indicated that ascertaining intention, knowledge and awareness of the parties was better left to courts, which were able to identify all relevant factors in a specific case. Concern was also expressed about the reference to "awareness", at least in some language versions.

218. After discussion, the Commission decided to delete article 7 and to address in the guide to enactment the issues covered in that article.

Article 8. Unexpected actions carried out by automated systems

219. It was noted that article 8 addressed an important issue associated with automated contracting using artificial intelligence systems, which were characterized by a lack of predictability. It was also noted that unexpected actions could occur throughout the contract life cycle, and that that should be reiterated in the guide to enactment in the same way as for other provisions (see para. 195 above).

220. The view was expressed that although article 8 should focus on unpredicted or unintended outputs of artificial intelligence systems owing to their inherent characteristics, it should also cover errors in programming and third-party interference. It was observed that those risks could be more prevalent in automated contracting compared with more traditional forms of electronic contracting on account of a wider range of technical issues outside the control of the user. It was suggested that the expanded coverage of the provision should be acknowledged in the draft guide to enactment. It was added that the expanded coverage could encourage better anti-fraud and risk management practices and greater transparency in the operation of artificial intelligence systems used for automated contracting.

221. Different views were expressed on the form and substance of article 8. One view was that the provision was unworkable in practice and risked upsetting fundamental principles of contract law, and should therefore be deleted entirely. It was recalled that the provision was inspired by a dissenting opinion in the case of *B2C2 Ltd. v. Quoine Pte. Ltd.* before the Court of Appeal of Singapore.[26] It was conceded that further research could be undertaken on existing legal solutions to unexpected actions. In that regard, rules on aleatory contracts and hardship were mentioned. It was noted that, in a business-to-business context, unexpected actions were ordinarily addressed in an agreement between the parties (e.g. a framework agreement); therefore, a new rule would add little value.

[26] Civil Appeal No. 81 of 2019, Judgment, 24 February 2020, Singapore Law Reports, vol. 2020, No. 2, p. 20, [2020] SGCA(I) 02.

222. Another view was that the provision provided a suitable solution and could be retained, subject to several improvements, to promote legal certainty and build confidence in the use of automated systems.

223. Firstly, it was suggested that the rule in paragraph 1 should be applied "in the light of all the circumstances". However, given the limitations on accessing information on automated systems (see para. 216) and the fact that such information might not be readily understood by users, the view was expressed that it was not appropriate to refer specifically to "the information made available to the parties on the design or operation of the system"; therefore, those words should not be retained in the chapeau of paragraph 1.

224. Secondly, it was observed that greater clarity was needed as to how to ascertain the expectations of the parties. The difficulties of ascertaining the subjective expectations of the parties, particularly in the context of machine-to-machine interactions, were stressed. Broad support was expressed for requiring the expectations of the parties and the term "reasonably" to be ascertained objectively. It was suggested that that should be clearly stated in the guide to enactment, along with a list of relevant circumstances for ascertaining those expectations, such as the nature and purpose of the contract and the usages and practices of the parties. It was added that the rule in paragraph 1 concerned the expectations of the parties at the time that the relevant action was carried out.

225. Thirdly, given that article 8 addressed a substantive law issue, it was suggested that paragraph 1 should refer to what the party relying on the action could reasonably be expected to have known, rather than what they "ought to have known".

226. Fourthly, it was queried whether it was appropriate for the rule in paragraph 1 to focus on whether an action was expected. It was added that the expectations of the parties ordinarily related to the benefits derived from a contract, and that it would be difficult to determine what the expectations of a party were with respect to individual actions carried out by an automated system. It was suggested that the rule could focus on what the parties might reasonably "foresee". It was also suggested that the rule should require the action to significantly deviate from what was expected. It was observed that unexpected actions referred to outcomes where the party would not have concluded the contract or would have done so only on fundamentally different contract terms should it have been aware of the action from the outset.

227. Another view was that the rule should be set out in the guide to enactment. Alternatively, the suggestion was made to formulate an optional provision for jurisdictions for which unexpected actions of automated systems posed challenges that could not be addressed under existing law or that warranted a specific solution. It was agreed that the provision of article 8 would only be optional, since its principle was still not accepted in various jurisdictions. Therefore, it was agreed that the text would be placed in square brackets to indicate its optional nature, and that that should be fully explained in the guide to enactment. The view was expressed that the enactment of article 8 depended on policy decisions regarding the allocation of risk and that guidance on the matter could be provided in the guide to enactment. It was noted that article 8 would need to depend on other law to provide solutions to evidentiary issues.

228. The Commission considered the suggestion, in footnote 21 of document A/CN.9/1178, to replace article 8 with a rule stating that attribution of an output of an automated system should not be denied on the sole ground that the party did not expect that output. Broad support was expressed for including such a rule to complement, rather than replace, article 8.

229. The Commission heard several drafting proposals as a basis for proceeding with its consideration of article 8. Since the rule in footnote 21concerned attribution, it was agreed that it should be placed in article 6 as its third paragraph, to read as follows: "Attribution of an action carried out by an automated system shall not be denied on the sole ground that the outcome was unexpected."

230. It was suggested that paragraph 2 (b) of article 8 should be retained as a stand-alone provision or inserted in article 2. It was also suggested that the provision should refer to information on the "use" of the system, mirroring amendments to article 2, and that the guide to enactment should clarify that the provision was not exhaustive of information requirements that might be imposed under other law. The Commission agreed to retain paragraph 2 (b) as a stand-alone provision entitled "information requirements" and to insert it after article 8 as follows: "Nothing in this Law affects the application of any rule of law that may require a person to disclose information on the design, operation or use of an automated system, or provides legal consequences for failing to do so or for disclosing inaccurate, incomplete or false information."

231. It was also suggested that paragraphs 1 and 2 should be amended by: (a) inserting wording along the lines of "unless the parties agree otherwise," at the beginning of the paragraph; (b) removing the square brackets but deleting the words "including the information made available to the parties on the design or operation of the system"; (c) replacing "ought" with "could reasonably be expected" in paragraph 1 (b); and (d) deleting in paragraph 2 (a) the words "other than as provided for in paragraph 1". Support was expressed for those proposals, as well as for reformulating paragraph 1 to clarify when it was referring to the party to which the action was attributed and when it was referring to the party seeking to rely on that action.

232. The Commission agreed to retain article 8 as an optional provision, to read as follows:

> "1. Unless otherwise agreed by the parties, where an action carried out by an automated system is attributed to a party to a contract, the other party to the contract is not entitled to rely on that action if, in the light of all the circumstances:
>
> (a) The party to which the action is attributed could not reasonably have expected the action; and
>
> (b) The other party knew or could reasonably be expected to have known that the party to which the action is attributed did not expect the action.
>
> "2. Nothing in this article affects the application of any rule of law or agreement of the parties that may govern the legal consequences of an action carried out by an automated system."

233. The Commission also agreed that article 8 should be presented in the final text in square brackets to identify it as an optional provision and that it should be accompanied by a footnote reading as follows: "This provision is included for States wishing to enact one or more specific provisions addressing unexpected actions carried out by automated systems."

Article 9. Non-avoidance

234. In response to a query, it was explained that the function of article 9 was not to allocate liability, but rather to ensure that the use of an automated system would not by itself be considered a reason not to perform a contract, or otherwise to comply with a rule of law.

235. It was suggested that the words "perform the contract" were unnecessary as the focus of the provision was compliance with a rule of law. Similarly, it was noted that the reference to the parties to the contract was superfluous, as all persons should comply with a rule of law when automated systems were used. It was also noted that the reference to the purpose for which the automated system was used was redundant, could inadvertently raise complex evidentiary issues and could be misconstrued as referring to an intention not to comply with the law. It was further suggested that the guide to enactment could refer to data protection and privacy laws as an illustration of the types of laws relevant to the article.

236. It was emphasized that removing the reference to "perform the contract" did not imply that an automated system could be used to justify contractual non-compliance, which in any event was captured by the reference to "failure to comply with a rule of law". After discussion, the Commission agreed to amend article 9 to read as follows: "Unless otherwise provided by law, a party shall not be relieved from the legal consequences of its failure to comply with a rule of law on the sole ground that it used an automated system."

Guide to enactment

237. In view of the amendments to the draft guide to enactment that were suggested during the discussions, as well as those necessary to reflect agreed amendments to the draft provisions, the Commission agreed to: (a) approve the guide to enactment in principle; (b) request the secretariat to finalize it to reflect the deliberations and decisions of the Commission; and (c) authorize Working Group IV to review the guide at its sixty-seventh session, in 2024. A proposal to allow the Working Group to finalize the text of the provisions at its next session did not receive support. It was said that a precedent should not be created with the Commission considering texts that have not been prior considered by the relevant Working Group.

C. Form

238. Although the view was expressed that it would be sufficient to adopt the provisions as a set of model legislative provisions, broad support was expressed for adopting the provisions in the form of a stand-alone model law. It was anticipated that some jurisdictions would enact the model law by incorporating its provisions into legislation enacting other UNCITRAL e-commerce texts such as the Model Law on Electronic Commerce or the Electronic Communications Convention. To complete the text, the Commission agreed to insert, after article 2, an interpretation provision formulated in the same terms as article 3 of the UNCITRAL Model Law on Electronic Commerce.

D. Adoption of the UNCITRAL Model Law on Automated Contracting

239. At its 1231st meeting, on 11 July 2024, the Commission adopted by consensus the following decision:

"*The United Nations Commission on International Trade Law*,

"*Recalling* its mandate under General Assembly resolution 2205 (XXI) of 17 December 1966 to further the progressive harmonization and unification of the law of international trade and in that respect to bear in mind the interests of all peoples, in particular those of developing countries, in the extensive development of international trade,

"*Recalling also* its decision at the fifty-fourth session, in 2021, to place the topic of automated contracting on its work programme,[27] and its decision at the fifty-fifth session, in 2022, to refer work on automated contracting to Working Group IV (Electronic Commerce), namely, as a first stage, to compile provisions of UNCITRAL texts that apply to automated contracting, and revise those provisions, as appropriate, and, as a second stage, to identify and develop possible new provisions,[28]

"*Mindful* that the UNCITRAL Model Law on the Use and Cross-border Recognition of Identity Management and Trust Services (2022),[29] the UNCITRAL

[27] *Official Records of the General Assembly, Seventy-sixth Session, Supplement No. 17* (A/76/17), paras. 25 (e) and 236.
[28] Ibid., *Seventy-seventh Session, Supplement No. 17* (A/77/17), para. 22 (d).
[29] Ibid., annex II.

Model Law on Electronic Transferable Records (2017),[30] the Electronic Communications Convention (2005),[31] the UNCITRAL Model Law on Electronic Signatures (2001)[32] and the UNCITRAL Model Law on Electronic Commerce (1996)[33] are of significant assistance to States in enabling and facilitating electronic commerce in international trade,

"*Mindful also* of the importance of providing a legal foundation for promoting confidence in electronic commerce, including across borders, and of the increasing relevance of automation in contracting, including through the deployment of artificial intelligence systems,

"*Considering* that uncertainty as to the legal effect of automation in contracting can create an obstacle to harnessing the full potential of digital trade,

"*Convinced* that legal certainty and commercial predictability in electronic commerce, including across borders, will be enhanced through the harmonization of certain rules on the use of automation in contracting on a technologically neutral basis and, where applied in conjunction with other harmonized rules on electronic contracting, when appropriate, according to the functional equivalence approach,

"*Having considered*, at its fifty-seventh session, in 2024, draft provisions on automated contracting[34] and an accompanying guide to enactment,[35]

"*Expressing* its appreciation to Working Group IV for its work on automated contracting,

"1. *Adopts* the UNCITRAL Model Law on Automated Contracting, as contained in annex IV to the report of the United Nations Commission on International Trade Law on the work of its fifty-seventh session;[36]

"2. *Approves* in principle the draft guide to enactment of the UNCITRAL Model Law on Automated Contracting, and requests the secretariat to finalize it by reflecting deliberations and decisions at the fifty-seventh session of the Commission, and authorizes Working Group IV (Electronic Commerce) to review the guide at its sixty-seventh session, in 2024;

"3. *Requests* the Secretary-General to publish the UNCITRAL Model Law on Automated Contracting together with a guide to enactment, including electronically, in the six official languages of the United Nations, and to disseminate it broadly to Governments and other interested bodies;

"4. *Recommends* that all States give favourable consideration to the UNCITRAL Model Law on Automated Contracting when revising or adopting legislation relevant to electronic contracting, and invites States that have used the Model Law to advise the Commission accordingly."

VIII. Investor-State dispute settlement reform: progress report of Working Group III

240. The Commission recalled that, at its fiftieth session, in 2017, it had entrusted Working Group III with a broad mandate to work on the possible reform of investor-State dispute settlement.[37] The Commission also recalled that, at its fifty-sixth session, in 2023, it had finalized and adopted the first set of investor-State dispute

[30] Ibid., *Seventy-second Session, Supplement No. 17* (A/72/17), annex I.
[31] General Assembly resolution 60/21, annex.
[32] General Assembly resolution 56/80, annex.
[33] General Assembly resolution 51/162, annex.
[34] A/CN.9/1178.
[35] A/CN.9/1179.
[36] *Official Records of the General Assembly, Seventy-ninth Session, Supplement No. 17* (A/79/17), annex IV.
[37] Ibid., *Seventy-second Session, Supplement No. 17* (A/72/17), para. 264.

settlement reform elements recommended by the Working Group.[38] It further recalled that the Working Group had been encouraged to submit to the Commission for consideration at the current session the outcome of its work on the draft provisions on an advisory centre on international investment law and a guidance text on means to prevent and mitigate disputes.[39]

241. Taking into account the reports of Working Group III on the work of its forty-sixth, forty-seventh and forty-eighth sessions (A/CN.9/1160, A/CN.9/1161 and A/CN.9/1167, respectively), the Commission commended the Working Group for completing its work on the statute of an advisory centre on international investment dispute resolution and noted the progress made with regard to a toolkit on prevention and mitigation of international investment disputes (see chap. VI for detailed consideration of those texts, as well as the way forward).

242. The Commission noted that progress was being made on other reform elements, including a number of procedural and cross-cutting issues, various aspects of a standing mechanism, an appellate mechanism and a multilateral instrument on investor-State dispute settlement reform. The Commission also noted that progress was being facilitated through a series of intersessional and other informal meetings.[40] In that context, reference was made to the sixth and seventh intersessional meetings, held in Singapore (September 2023) and Brussels (March 2024), respectively. Furthermore, it was mentioned that the eighth intersessional meeting of Working Group III was scheduled to be held in Chengdu, China, on 24 and 25 October 2024, on topics relating to an appellate mechanism and a multilateral instrument on investor-State dispute settlement reform, and that the ninth intersessional meeting was scheduled to be held in Seoul in early March 2025, on procedural and cross-cutting issues (A/CN.9/1167, para. 115). It was reaffirmed that no decisions would be taken at those meetings.

243. The Commission expressed its appreciation to the secretariat for closely cooperating with the Advisory Centre on World Trade Organization Law on the advisory centre and with the World Bank Group on the topic of dispute prevention and mitigation. The Commission also commended the secretariat for its participation in events organized by UNCTAD, the International Centre for Settlement of Investment Disputes, the Organisation for Economic Co-operation and Development (OECD) and UNIDROIT, as well as for coordinating generally with international governmental and non-governmental organizations to hold a number of side events on a range of topics during the sessions of the Working Group.

244. The Commission recalled that the General Assembly, on 24 December 2021, had decided to allocate an additional one-week session per year to the Commission and the necessary human resources to the secretariat to support the work of Working Group III.[41] The Commission further recalled that, when it had made the recommendation to the General Assembly for the additional resources, it had decided to re-evaluate and, if needed, revisit its decision concerning the need for allocating an additional one-week session per year and supporting resources to the Working Group, taking into consideration the Working Group's report on the use of its resources.[42]

245. Accordingly, the Commission was informed that the additional conference time of one week allocated for 2024 had been utilized by the Working Group to hold a one-week forty-seventh session in Vienna in January 2024.[43] It was observed that the

---

[38] Ibid., *Seventy-eighth Session, Supplement No. 17* (A/78/17), chap. IV.

[39] Ibid., para. 151.

[40] Information about informal meetings is available on the web page of Working Group III (https://uncitral.un.org/en/working_groups/3/investor-state) in the right-hand column under "Inter-sessional Activities".

[41] General Assembly resolution 76/229, para. 15.

[42] *Official Records of the General Assembly, Seventy-sixth Session, Supplement No. 17* (A/76/17), para. 263.

[43] Ibid., *Seventy-eighth Session, Supplement No. 17* (A/78/17), para. 315.

additional conference time had allowed the Working Group to complete its consideration of the draft statute of an advisory centre on international investment dispute resolution. The Commission was further informed that two of the three additional posts allocated in 2022 were being utilized, while one of the posts, which was vacant as a result of the secondment of the staff member, could not be filled owing to the liquidity crisis affecting the United Nations Secretariat and the consequent hiring restrictions. Lastly, the Commission was informed that the allocation of additional resources by the General Assembly to support the work of Working Group III was expected to end in 2025.

246. The Chair of Working Group III provided an outline of the work to be conducted by the Working Group during the three weeks of sessions scheduled until the fifty-eighth session of the Commission and indicated that the Working Group would aim to submit proposals regarding reforms relating to procedural and cross-cutting issues and a draft statute on a standing mechanism for consideration by the Commission at its next session.

247. The Commission reiterated that progress should continue to be made in accordance with the revised workplan prepared by the Working Group at its resumed fortieth session, in May 2021 (A/CN.9/1054, annex). While emphasizing the need to take a flexible approach in carrying out the work and adapt the workplan to the current needs of the Working Group, the Commission requested the Working Group to continue its work in an effective manner and encouraged it to present the outcome of the above-mentioned work at its next session, in 2025.

248. The Commission further noted the outreach activities of the secretariat aimed at raising awareness about the work of the Working Group and ensuring that the process would remain inclusive and fully transparent. The Commission also commended the secretariat for updating the Working Group III web page to provide relevant information to delegates in a concise and timely manner.

249. The Commission expressed its appreciation for the financial support provided by the Governments of France and Germany, the European Union and the Swiss Agency for Development and Cooperation. The Commission called for continued support by donors for travel and simultaneous interpretation to ensure the inclusiveness of the Working Group deliberations, and for post-related costs to enhance the capacities of the secretariat.

250. After discussion, the Commission expressed its satisfaction with the progress made by Working Group III and the support provided by the secretariat to the Working Group.

IX. Electronic commerce: progress report of Working Group IV

251. The Commission recalled that, at its fifty-fifth session, in 2022, it had mandated Working Group IV to proceed with work on data provision contracts in tandem with work on the use of artificial intelligence and automation in contracting.[44] At the present session, the Commission had before it the report of the Working Group on the work of its sixty-sixth session (Vienna, 16–20 October 2023) (A/CN.9/1162). It was reported that that session had largely been devoted to work on automated contracting, which the Commission had finalized at the present session, and included consideration of a proposal to consolidate UNCITRAL texts on electronic transactions (A/CN.9/1162, paras. 90–92). The Commission expressed its satisfaction with the progress made by the Working Group.

[44] Ibid., *Seventy-seventh Session, Supplement No. 17* (A/77/17), para. 163.

X. Insolvency law: progress report of Working Group V

252. The Commission had before it the reports of Working Group V on the work of its sixty-third session (Vienna, 11–15 December 2023) (A/CN.9/1163) and sixty-fourth session (New York, 13–17 May 2024) (A/CN.9/1169) and noted with appreciation the progress made by the Working Group in its consideration of the topics of asset tracing and recovery and applicable law in insolvency proceedings at those sessions. It commended the Working Group and the secretariat for continuing to treat both topics equally, in accordance with the mandate given to the Working Group,[45] and for the high quality of the documents prepared by the secretariat for those sessions.

253. With regard to the topic of asset tracing and recovery, the Commission was informed that at those sessions, the Working Group had completed its review of the second and third drafts of a text on asset tracing and recovery in insolvency proceedings (A/CN.9/WG.V/WP.189 and A/CN.9/WG.V/WP.192) and of a draft toolkit for expedited asset tracing and recovery in insolvency proceedings (A/CN.9/WG.V/WP.189, appendix I, and A/CN.9/WG.V/WP.193). Furthermore, it was informed that the Working Group should be ready to transmit both texts, as revised at those sessions and possibly also at the next two sessions of the Working Group, for consideration and finalization by the Commission at its fifty-eighth session, in 2025. The Commission noted that support had been expressed in the Working Group for omitting the word "civil" in the titles of those texts and of the prevailing view in the Working Group that: (a) the text in its final form should be called "Background notes on asset tracing and recovery in insolvency proceedings"; (b) the toolkit in its final form should be called "Toolkit for expedited asset tracing and recovery in insolvency proceedings"; and (c) those two separate parts could be grouped together under the heading: "Asset tracing and recovery in insolvency proceedings: toolkit and background notes" (A/CN.9/1169, paras. 38 and 39). With a view to ensuring that the final UNCITRAL product on the topic was of practical value, it was suggested that the toolkit should be featured first and more prominently in the final text, accompanied by the background notes, in the same way that recommendations were accompanied by a commentary in UNCITRAL legislative guides.

254. With regard to the topic of applicable law in insolvency proceedings, the Commission noted that the Working Group had continued to consider draft legislative provisions and commentary, which had been expanded to cover cross-border recognition and enforcement aspects and possible additional exceptions to the *lex fori concursus* rule. The Commission encouraged the Working Group to resolve outstanding issues as soon as possible, while at the same time recognizing that those issues were complex and contentious, requiring further extensive consultations before an acceptable solution could be reached.

255. Views differed on how Working Group V could benefit from the views of arbitration experts on outstanding arbitration-related questions, as well as on whether coordination with Working Group II would be at all necessary, useful or productive on those questions, and if so, how it could be arranged. Although there was some support for coordination with Working Group II on a few arbitration-related aspects that remained to be discussed in the applicable law project of Working Group V, the view prevailed that the efficient coordination of insolvency and arbitration aspects could be achieved at the delegation and secretariat levels, for example by including arbitration and insolvency experts in delegations at Working Group V sessions or ensuring prior internal consultations among those experts before Working Group V sessions.

[45] Ibid., *Seventy-sixth Session, Supplement No. 17* (A/76/17), para. 217.

256. With reference to the secretariat's plans to update the *UNCITRAL Practice Guide on Cross-border Insolvency Cooperation*[46] (A/CN.9/1180, table 2 (a)) and support for those plans expressed by the Working Group (A/CN.9/1169, para. 90), the Commission requested the secretariat to update the *Practice Guide*, resources permitting and in consultation with relevant experts. The Commission requested the secretariat to present an updated text for review by the Working Group before transmitting it to the Commission for consideration and finalization. The understanding was that the updated *Practice Guide*, as approved by the Working Group and adopted by the Commission, would be published, like the original text, including electronically, in the six official languages of the United Nations and disseminated broadly so as to make it generally known and available, including for use in judicial capacity-building activities of the secretariat, its partners and other interested stakeholders.

XI. Negotiable cargo documents: progress report of Working Group VI

257. The Commission recalled that, at its fifty-fifth session, in 2022, it had decided to assign the topic of negotiable multimodal transport documents to Working Group VI.[47] The Working Group had commenced its deliberations on the basis of a set of preliminary draft provisions for an instrument on negotiable cargo documents prepared by the secretariat. The instrument was intended to enable the issuance of documents of title representing goods received for international carriage irrespective of the actual modes of transportation used for the particular carriage, which would be used for financing purposes. At the present session, the Commission had before it the reports of Working Group VI on the work of its forty-third session (Vienna, 27 November–1 December 2023) (A/CN.9/1164) and forty-fourth session (New York, 6–10 May 2024) (A/CN.9/1170).

258. The Commission noted that, at its fifty-sixth session, in 2023, it had reiterated the need to ensure a consistency of approach not only with existing instruments, such as the Model Law on Electronic Transferable Records,[48] but also among various projects that included electronic commerce aspects, such as the joint UNCITRAL-UNIDROIT Model Law on Warehouse Receipts. The Commission was informed that Working Group VI had completed its review of draft chapter 3 on negotiable electronic cargo records and requested the secretariat to align draft provisions more closely with the Model Law on Electronic Transferable Records. Working Group VI had also agreed to follow the approach to electronic aspects adopted in the draft joint UNCITRAL-UNIDROIT model law on warehouse receipts.

259. The Commission noted that, during its forty-fourth session, Working Group VI had heard presentations by the Intergovernmental Organisation for International Carriage by Rail, the Organisation for Co-operation between Railways and the International Civil Aviation Organization on the issuance and use of non-negotiable transport documents under the Uniform Rules concerning the Contract of International Carriage of Goods by Rail, the Agreement on International Railway Freight Communications and the Convention for the Unification of Certain Rules for International Carriage by Air, with a view to identifying possible conflicts between the draft instrument and existing transport law conventions. In that respect, it was pointed out that draft article 7 (Extent of rights of the holder under a negotiable cargo document) of the instrument explicitly provided that the holder would acquire all

[46] United Nations publication, Sales No.: E.10.V.6, available at https://uncitral.un.org/en/texts/insolvency/explanatorytexts/practice_guide_cross-border_insolvency.

[47] *Official Records of the General Assembly, Seventy-seventh Session, Supplement No. 17* (A/77/17), para. 202.

[48] Ibid., *Seventy-eighth Session, Supplement No. 17* (A/78/17), para. 170.

rights under the transport contract and that any entitlement to such rights conferred upon the consignor or the consignee would extinguish (A/CN.9/WG.VI/WP.103).

260. The Commission also noted the holding of two side events during the forty-fourth session of the Working Group focusing on an enabling legal environment for digital transport and on industry perspectives on the future impact of negotiable cargo documents and negotiable electronic cargo records. Speakers at those side events included key international industry representatives of shippers, commodity traders, banks, freight forwarders, maritime, rail and air carriers and insurers. It was noted, inter alia, that the flexibility to sell goods to another buyer while they were in transit was becoming an important part of efforts by shippers to build resilience into supply chains at times of disruption.

261. The Commission was informed that significant progress had been made on the draft instrument on negotiable cargo documents and that Working Group VI might be in a position to transmit the draft instrument to the Commission for its review and possible adoption at its next session, in 2025. The Commission expressed its satisfaction with the progress made by the Working Group and the support provided by the secretariat. At the same time, the Commission heard a concern that the draft instrument, like the newly adopted Model Law on Warehouse Receipts, contained provisions on matters addressed in the Model Law on Electronic Transferable Records and that a better approach might have been to recommend to States the adoption of the latter Model Law instead. The need to adequately address any potential conflicts with existing transport law conventions was emphasized in that regard. The Commission was sympathetic to that concern but was of the view that a decision on whether or not to include provisions on documents in electronic form had to be taken for each instrument on an individual basis, taking into account its purpose and form. The Commission nevertheless emphasized the need to avoid duplication of work and to ensure consistency with existing UNCITRAL texts on electronic commerce, in particular the Model Law on Electronic Transferable Records. In that respect, the Commission heard a suggestion that the draft instrument should contain an explanation of how it could be applied in States that had already enacted laws based on the Model Law on Electronic Transferable Records.

262. The Commission concluded its deliberations by reiterating its belief in the usefulness of the project. It invited States and relevant organizations to actively participate in the development of the new instrument on negotiable cargo documents.

XII. Work programme

263. The Commission recalled its agreement to reserve time for discussion of its overall work programme as a separate topic at each session, to facilitate the effective planning of its activities.[49]

264. The Commission took note of the documents prepared to assist its discussions on the topic (A/CN.9/1180 and the documents referred to therein, including the proposals contained in documents A/CN.9/1175, A/CN.9/1189, A/CN.9/1190 and A/CN.9/1191) and of lists of activities of the secretariat planned until the fifty-eighth session of the Commission in support of the legislative work by the Commission and its working groups.

A. Legislative programme under consideration by working groups

265. The Commission noted the progress of its working groups as reported earlier in the session (see chaps. VIII to XI of the present report) and reaffirmed the programme

[49] Ibid., *Sixty-eighth Session, Supplement No. 17* (A/68/17), para. 310.

of current legislative activities set out in table 1 of document A/CN.9/1180, as follows:

(a) The Commission authorized the secretariat to utilize part of the conference time tentatively allocated to Working Group I in the second half of 2024 and the first half of 2025 for colloquiums (see sects. B.1 (b) to C.1 of the present chapter);

(b) With respect to dispute settlement, the Commission requested Working Group II to edit and finalize the draft explanatory notes to the UNCITRAL Model Clauses on Specialized Express Dispute Resolution, and further mandated the Working Group to work on the recognition and enforcement of electronic arbitral awards and, subsequently, on electronic notices;

(c) With respect to investor-State dispute settlement reform, the Commission agreed that Working Group III should continue with its work programme as mandated;

(d) With respect to electronic commerce, the Commission confirmed that Working Group IV should continue to work on the formulation of default rules on data provision contracts and would review the guide to enactment of the model law on automated contracting as adopted by the Commission at the present session;

(e) With respect to insolvency law, the Commission agreed that Working Group V should continue its consideration of legal issues arising from asset tracing and recovery in insolvency proceedings, as well as the topic of applicable law in insolvency proceedings;

(f) With respect to negotiable cargo documents (previously referred to as "negotiable multimodal transport documents"), the Commission agreed that Working Group VI should continue its consideration of a new international instrument on negotiable cargo documents.

B. Additional topics considered at earlier sessions of the Commission

1. Climate change mitigation, adaptation and resilience

266. The Commission recalled that, at its fifty-fourth session, in 2021, it had heard a proposal to examine (a) how existing UNCITRAL texts could be aligned with climate change mitigation, adaptation and resilience goals, and (b) whether further work could be done by UNCITRAL to facilitate those goals in the implementation of those texts or through the development of new texts. It had been added that public-private partnerships could be an area of focus for taking stock of existing texts, while legal uncertainty regarding the legal status of carbon credits traded in voluntary carbon markets could be a focus for future legislative work.[50]

267. Broad support had been expressed at that time for the Commission to consider the proposal further, based on more precise information on the work involved. After discussion, the Commission had requested the secretariat to consult with interested States with a view to developing a more detailed proposal on the topic for presentation to the Commission for its consideration at its next session, in 2022.[51]

268. The Commission recalled that, at its fifty-fifth session, in 2022, it had considered a note by the Secretariat summarizing the findings and recommendations of a study on private law aspects of climate change commissioned from an outside expert with a view to assisting the Commission in considering the desirability and feasibility of undertaking work in that area (A/CN.9/1120 and A/CN.9/1120/Add.1). At that time, there had been wide agreement within the Commission on the importance of the topic and the usefulness of exploring how UNCITRAL could offer its own contribution to the international community's efforts to combat climate change and mitigate its effects by updating existing private law instruments and developing new enabling

[50] Ibid., *Seventy-sixth Session, Supplement No. 17* (A/76/17), para. 244.

[51] Ibid., para. 246.

legal mechanisms, if necessary.[52] The Commission had requested the secretariat to conduct further research in the area, in consultation with outside experts and interested organizations from both within and outside the United Nations system.[53] It had also requested the secretariat to organize a colloquium or an expert group meeting on the various legal issues surrounding climate change mitigation, adaptation and resilience, in conjunction with relevant and interested international organizations.[54]

269. The Commission further recalled the UNCITRAL Colloquium on Climate Change and International Trade Law, which had been held during its fifty-sixth session, in 2023, to consider areas in which international trade law could effectively support the achievement of climate action goals set by the international community, the scope and value of legal harmonization in those areas and the need for international guidance for legislators, policymakers, courts and dispute resolution bodies. The Commission noted that the Colloquium had consisted of seven panels involving over 30 speakers and moderators from international intergovernmental and non-governmental organizations, industry and business representatives, academia and private practice from all continents.[55] The Commission had noted the main topics discussed and the proposals for future work made at the Colloquium and had further considered a note by the Secretariat on the subject (A/CN.9/1153 and A/CN.9/1153/Add.1), which had provided additional information and comments received by the secretariat on the issues discussed in the note that the Commission had considered at its fifty-fifth session (A/CN.9/1120 and A/CN.9/1120/Add.1).

270. The Commission recalled that, at the fifty-sixth session, there had been wide agreement on the usefulness of a mapping exercise of relevant questions of international trade law, private law and private international law.[56] There had also been wide support within the Commission for the need to ensure consistency and inclusiveness and to avoid overlap and duplication of international efforts in that area.[57] After discussion, the Commission had requested the secretariat to: (a) within the mandate of UNCITRAL, consult with all States Members of the United Nations with a view to developing a more detailed study on the aspects of international trade law related to voluntary carbon credits; (b) include in the study consideration of outputs from other relevant forums and processes, including the United Nations Framework Convention on Climate Change Conference (UNFCCC), and whether UNCITRAL efforts would be redundant; (c) conduct the study in cooperation and collaboration with UNFCCC, UNIDROIT, the Hague Conference on Private International Law (HCCH) and other organizations with relevant expertise; (d) invite all States Members of the United Nations to nominate experts to provide input to the work of the secretariat in that area; (e) aim for as wide representation as possible, in particular representation from developing countries; (f) make the study available well in advance of its fifty-seventh session and provide an opportunity for all States Members of the United Nations to submit views and comments on the study; and (g) submit the study, as well as a compilation of the views and comments received from States, in advance of its fifty-seventh session.[58]

271. At the present session, the Commission had before it a note by the Secretariat on the UNCITRAL-UNIDROIT study on the legal nature of verified carbon credits issued by independent carbon standard setters (A/CN.9/1191). The Commission also based its discussion on the note by the Secretariat on the work programme of the Commission (A/CN.9/1180, paras. 8–18).

---

[52] Ibid., *Seventy-seventh Session, Supplement No. 17* (A/77/17), para. 212.
[53] Ibid., para. 216.
[54] Ibid.
[55] Ibid., *Seventy-eighth Session, Supplement No. 17* (A/78/17), para. 191.
[56] Ibid., para. 193.
[57] Ibid., para. 195.
[58] Ibid., para. 199.

(a) UNCITRAL-UNIDROIT study on the legal nature of verified carbon credits issued by independent carbon standard setters

272. The Commission commended the secretariat for having prepared the UNCITRAL-UNIDROIT study on the legal nature of verified carbon credits issued by independent carbon standard setters, which provided more detailed information on the aspects of international trade law related to verified carbon credits. The Commission further commended the secretariat for having: (a) consulted with all States Members of the United Nations through a questionnaire on carbon markets and carbon credits circulated on 6 October 2023, and with State-nominated experts; and (b) cooperated and collaborated with the secretariats of UNFCCC, UNIDROIT, HCCH and other organizations with relevant expertise in order to advance the preparation of the study.

273. The Commission noted with satisfaction the abundant sources of information considered in the study, including States' replies to the questionnaire, comments from State-nominated experts, the UNIDROIT Work Programme on the Legal Nature of Verified Carbon Credits, UNIDROIT issue papers and working group discussions, the discussions at the Joint Meeting of the UNCITRAL Expert Group and the UNIDROIT Working Group on the Legal Nature of Voluntary Carbon Credits (31 January and 1 February 2024) and reports on the same topic prepared by relevant stakeholders, such as the International Organization of Securities Commissions, the International Swaps and Derivatives Association, OECD and the World Bank Group.

274. The Commission thanked those States, the majority of which were developing countries, that had contributed to the study either by transmitting their reply to the questionnaire or by nominating experts to provide input. The Commission stressed the usefulness of the study, including for countries that were currently considering enacting legislation in the area, but noted that the stringent timeline for preparing the study and processing its translation had not permitted its circulation for comments by all Member States ahead of the present session. Noting also that the study was already available in the six official languages of the United Nations on the Commission web page, the Commission requested the secretariat to circulate it to all States Members of the United Nations and give them sufficient time to provide the secretariat with their technical and editorial comments, with a view to compiling those comments and submitting them, together with the study, in its current form, for consideration at its fifty-eighth session, in 2025. The Commission agreed to hold a further discussion during that session on the findings of the study, as well as the issues highlighted by States in their comments, and to consider at that stage whether to request the secretariat to prepare a revised version of the study, taking into account the Commission's deliberations and the comments received, for publication after that session.

(b) Future work deliberations at the Commission

275. The Commission noted the suggestion that some of the topics other than the legal nature of verified carbon credits discussed at the Colloquium held at its fifty-sixth session, in 2023, might merit further exploration with a view to possible future work. Those topics included the following: (a) international, regional and State efforts to call upon private sector support to achieve climate goals by advocating and advancing climate-responsible corporate conduct; (b) various adaptation strategies and approaches available to private sector operators to promote sustainability in their supply chains; (c) current trends in climate change disputes and their legal implication for corporate entities to fulfil their duty of care and foster the incorporation of climate considerations into business and investment decisions; and (d) the relevance of UNCITRAL instruments to climate action.

276. The Commission was informed that the secretariat could hold a two-day colloquium to examine those topics and conduct further exploratory work on the subject. The Commission was also informed that the meeting hours would be shortened if online interventions from speakers were to be expected. The Commission

was of the view that any further consideration of those topics should, for the time being, focus only on the relevance of UNCITRAL instruments to climate action, notably, the United Nations Convention on Contracts for the International Sale of Goods (United Nations Sales Convention (1980)),[59] the UNCITRAL Model Law on Public Procurement,[60] the UNCITRAL Model Legislative Provisions on Public-Private Partnerships[61] and the instruments on dispute settlement, with a view to assessing the need for the secretariat or a working group to prepare guidance documents on the practical application and interpretation of existing instruments and possible supplementary texts to address issues concerning climate action. After discussion, the Commission requested the secretariat to organize a two-day colloquium in a hybrid format, with a focus on the relevance of UNCITRAL instruments to climate action and, for that purpose, authorized the secretariat to utilize conference time tentatively allocated to Working Group I in the second half of 2024.

2. Dispute resolution in the digital economy

277. The Commission recalled that, at its fifty-sixth session, in 2023, it had requested the secretariat to continue to implement the project on the stocktaking of developments in dispute resolution in the digital economy, as endorsed at its fifty-fourth session, in 2021, including the "world tour", to put forward proposals for possible legislative work with a focus on the topics of the recognition and enforcement of electronic awards and electronic notices of arbitration and their delivery, and to report on further progress made overall.[62]

278. At the present session, the Commission had before it notes by the Secretariat containing a progress report and future work proposals related to the stocktaking of developments in dispute resolution in the digital economy (A/CN.9/1189 and A/CN.9/1190). The Commission noted that, in response to its request, the progress report contained a summary of the "world tour" discussions organized to obtain input from practitioners, academics and stakeholders across regions and, on the basis of those discussions, the note on future work proposals presented proposals on the two topics mentioned above and suggested areas for further exploratory work and monitoring. It was informed that the Government of Japan, through its Ministry of Justice, had contributed $415,175 for an additional period of 12 months to implement the stocktaking project. The Commission expressed its gratitude to the Government of Japan for its generous contribution and for its willingness to continue to support the project.

279. As to further exploratory work to be conducted under the stocktaking project, general support was expressed for providing the secretariat with flexibility to select relevant topics. The view was nonetheless expressed that further monitoring should not directly lead to new work proposals on platform-based dispute resolution, since UNCITRAL had already adopted the Technical Notes on Online Dispute Resolution. Furthermore, it was suggested that, since the field of artificial intelligence was rapidly evolving, although continued monitoring could be useful, efforts should instead focus on developing practical guidance for online hearings.

280. As outlined in paragraphs 83 to 85 of the note on future work proposals (A/CN.9/1190), the Commission considered the next steps based on the findings of the stocktaking exercise. In conjunction, it also took note of and considered the submission by the Governments of Germany, Israel, Japan, the Republic of Korea and Spain (A/CN.9/1186).

---

[59] United Nations, Treaty Series, vol. 1489, No. 25567, p. 3.

[60] *Official Records of the General Assembly, Sixty-sixth Session, Supplement No. 17* (A/66/17), annex I.

[61] Ibid., *Seventy-fourth Session, Supplement No. 17* (A/74/17), annex I.

[62] Ibid., *Seventy-eighth Session, Supplement No. 17* (A/78/17), para. 215.

281. There was broad support for the proposal to mandate a working group to proceed with work on the recognition and enforcement of electronic arbitral awards and, after the completion of that work, to work on the topic of electronic notices of arbitration.

282. With regard to the work on electronic awards, it was widely felt that the mandate of the working group should be broad and provide for flexibility to allow for the exploration of various approaches to facilitate the reliance on electronic awards without prejudice to the final form of the work.

283. It was emphasized that UNCITRAL texts in the area of electronic commerce, in particular the Electronic Communications Convention, should be considered to ensure consistency across UNCITRAL instruments and to capitalize on the solutions they provided.

Conclusion and way forward

284. After discussion, the Commission noted with great appreciation the work carried out by the secretariat and the notes by the Secretariat containing a progress report and future work proposals, and requested the secretariat to continue to implement the project to further monitor and explore relevant topics such as those related to artificial intelligence and platform-based dispute resolution, in collaboration with the Inclusive Global Legal Innovation Platform on Online Dispute Resolution.

285. Furthermore, the Commission mandated Working Group II to work on the recognition and enforcement of electronic arbitral awards and, subsequently, on electronic notices. In that regard, the Commission provided the Working Group with a broad mandate to identify the issues and explore appropriate solutions to those issues without prejudice to the final form of the outcome. In that connection, the Commission requested the secretariat to organize a two-day colloquium during the eightieth session of the Working Group with the aim of obtaining perspectives in order to further assess the issues with respect to electronic awards and further contemplate possible solutions for electronic notices of arbitration. The Commission further requested the secretariat to conduct preparatory work for the topic of the recognition and enforcement of electronic arbitral awards for consideration by the Working Group.

3. Consideration of legal issues relating to the use of distributed ledger technology in trade

286. The Commission recalled that, at its fifty-fifth session, in 2022, it had requested the secretariat to prepare a guidance document on legal issues relating to the use of distributed ledger systems in trade,[63] the purpose of which was to provide explanations useful to commercial operators, especially micro-, small and medium-sized enterprises and operators located in developing countries, in assessing whether distributed ledger technology-enabled services addressed their needs, and the impact of the use of such services on their business.[64]

287. The Commission also recalled that, at its fifty-sixth session, in 2023, it had considered a note by the Secretariat (A/CN.9/1146) that discussed the scope of the work to be conducted. On that occasion, broad support was expressed for the work to be carried out in close coordination with other concerned international organizations.[65]

288. At the present session, the Commission had before it a note by the secretariat on legal issues relating to the use of distributed ledger technology in trade (A/CN.9/1175). It was indicated that the note usefully established a link between distributed ledger technology and UNCITRAL texts and that the glossary was particularly valuable.

289. Broad support was expressed for the secretariat to continue its work, including in cooperation with other organizations. It was suggested that the work should focus

[63] Ibid., *Seventy-seventh Session, Supplement No. 17* (A/77/17), paras. 22 (f) and 169.
[64] Ibid., para. 167.
[65] Ibid., *Seventy-eighth Session, Supplement No. 17* (A/78/17), para. 201.

on areas in which UNCITRAL was active, such as security interests and tokenization of assets.

290. After discussion, the Commission requested the secretariat to continue and finalize its work on a guidance document on legal issues relating to the use of distributed ledger systems in trade, within existing resources, and in cooperation with other organizations, as appropriate.

C. Additional topics discussed at the present session

1. Secured transactions using new types of assets and their treatment under the UNCITRAL Model Law on Secured Transactions

291. The Commission recalled that, at its forty-ninth session, in 2016, it had adopted the UNCITRAL Model Law on Secured Transactions to support legislative reforms by States in the area of security interests with the aim of increasing access to affordable secured credit and promoting economic growth, sustainable development and financial inclusion.[66] It was noted that the Model Law dealt with security rights in all types of tangible and intangible movable property, providing a set of generic rules applicable to all types of assets, as well as certain asset-specific rules.

292. The Commission based its discussion on the note by the Secretariat on the work programme of the Commission (A/CN.9/1180, paras. 19–35). In light of the emergence of new types of assets (including digital assets, data, verified carbon credits and crop receipts) and legislative efforts by international and regional organizations to address transactions involving such assets, it was widely felt that it would be beneficial to compile information about those developments. Support was also expressed for taking stock of the enactment by States of the UNCITRAL Model Law on Secured Transactions and the approach taken by those States with regard to new types of assets, as well as of international financing practices using such assets.

293. It was, however, pointed out that the financing practices and the legislative approaches of States were still evolving, and that those practices and approaches were also based on different approaches to how to legally characterize those new types of assets. It was suggested that efforts should be made to compile and reflect on ongoing work that had been conducted by other international organizations to avoid any overlap. It was further suggested that the stocktaking should not be based on the assumption that the Model Law would necessarily need to be updated or amended, as it might be found to adequately address and apply equally to secured transactions involving new types of assets.

294. After discussion, the Commission considered it timely to address the above-mentioned developments with regard to the UNCITRAL Model Law on Secured Transactions with a view to assisting States with how to address secured transactions generally and those involving new types of assets in particular. It was agreed that such exploratory work would assist the Commission in making an informed decision on any possible future work, including any updates to the Model Law.

295. In that regard, the secretariat was requested to take stock of legislative developments related to new types of assets and the secured transaction laws of States to examine how the Model Law had been implemented. In addition, the secretariat was requested to organize a two- or three-day colloquium involving experts and representatives of international and regional organizations to clarify and refine various aspects of possible future work in the area and report back to the Commission at its fifty-eighth session, in 2025. It was suggested that the colloquium should be held in a hybrid format to enable remote participation.

[66] Ibid., *Seventy-first Session, Supplement No. 17* (A/71/17), para. 119.

2. Electronic commerce and paperless trade

296. The Commission heard a proposal for the secretariat to conduct a stocktaking exercise to examine all UNCITRAL texts that referred to electronic aspects, including UNCITRAL texts on electronic commerce and other substantive law texts that included provisions on electronic aspects (for example, the United Nations Convention on Contracts for the International Carriage of Goods Wholly or Partly by Sea, the UNCITRAL-UNIDROIT Model Law on Warehouse Receipts and the draft instrument on negotiable cargo documents). The outcome could be a comprehensive and systematic presentation of the stocktaking exercise that would clearly identify the scope of each instrument, its status, and the modality of adoption and enactment by States.

297. The Commission also heard proposals for the secretariat to: (a) initiate a stocktaking study on the possibility of systematizing and updating the UNCITRAL model legislation on paperless trade issues based on an assessment of existing UNCITRAL texts; (b) prepare a questionnaire on national experience within the existing legal framework on paperless trade, needs and tools for ensuring trust in cross-border trade relations, as well as in related areas of international cooperation, for example, in transport, finance and dispute resolution; and (c) hold a colloquium on the sidelines of a Working Group IV session on current topics related to the potential development of a universal paperless trade act. It was suggested that the exploratory work could result in a proposal to develop a single harmonized instrument covering the legal aspects of paperless trade.

298. Broad support was expressed for the proposals. It was said that the suggested exercises, which were to some extent complementary, could be useful not only in promoting the adoption and use of UNCITRAL texts, but also in identifying opportunities to update and complement those texts. In particular, it was noted that paperless trade was data-driven, and research in that field could provide useful input for other UNCITRAL projects. It was suggested that emerging issues such as the use of platforms by micro-, small and medium-sized enterprises should be explored. However, it was agreed that a step-by-step approach was desirable, and that the work should neither duplicate nor interfere with other ongoing projects.

299. After discussion, the Commission agreed to request the secretariat to conduct a stocktaking exercise to examine all UNCITRAL texts that referred to electronic aspects, including UNCITRAL texts on electronic commerce and other substantive law texts that included provisions on electronic aspects as described in paragraph 296 above. The Commission also requested that the stocktaking exercise include a survey of the incorporation by States of UNCITRAL texts on electronic commerce into their domestic legislation and the inclusion of such texts in international commitments concerning paperless trade. In that regard, the secretariat was requested to circulate a questionnaire, prepared with the help of experts, as needed, inviting States to provide information on the enactment or adoption of UNCITRAL texts on electronic commerce and to submit copies of their laws based on those texts, in particular those relevant to paperless trade. The secretariat was further requested to coordinate with other relevant organizations in the field of paperless trade, such as the Economic and Social Commission for Asia and the Pacific, UNCTAD, the United Nations Centre for Trade Facilitation and Electronic Business and the International Chamber of Commerce, as appropriate, and to present the results of the stocktaking exercise to the Commission for its consideration at a forthcoming session. The secretariat was requested to make the results of the stocktaking available to members and interested parties in an electronic and user-friendly format. In the view of the Commission, such results would assist the Commission in deciding on the next steps with respect to the contribution of UNCITRAL texts on electronic commerce to paperless trade and to decide whether further work was needed to prepare a document consolidating UNCITRAL texts on electronic transactions (see para. 251 above), with a particular focus on supporting paperless trade.

D. Working methods of UNCITRAL

(a) General comments

300. The Commission heard a suggestion that future Commission sessions should be organized in such a manner that all agenda items on policy issues (such as the work programme of the Commission) and housekeeping matters would be considered during the same week, rather than being spread over different weeks.

(b) Streamlining General Assembly resolutions on UNCITRAL annual reports

301. The Commission recalled that, at its fifty-sixth session, in 2023, it had considered a proposal for streamlining future UNCITRAL omnibus resolutions, and had requested the secretariat to facilitate an open and flexible intersessional consultative process among Member States with a view to developing guidelines on streamlining and simplifying the text of such resolutions and to report back thereon to the Commission at its next session, in 2024.[67]

302. The Commission noted that the secretariat had convened an informal consultation in Vienna on 12 June 2024 and that various views had been expressed on the proposed guiding principles discussed at its fifty-sixth session, in 2023.[68] The Commission heard from the secretariat that, at that informal consultation, which had been led by Panama, there was general support for the objective of streamlining UNCITRAL omnibus resolutions, namely, to enhance their user-friendliness, visibility and relevance to awareness-raising efforts by States and the secretariat relating to the work of UNCITRAL. The Commission noted a suggestion made at that informal consultation to integrate into the proposed guiding principles elements such as reorganizing and clustering information, ensuring coherence and avoiding repetition, as well as inserting thematic headings for groups of paragraphs on different thematic topics. The Commission also noted the view expressed that the guiding principles should preserve flexibility and that some of the proposed guiding principles, such as the principle on limiting reference to past events, were overly prescriptive.

303. In the ensuing discussion, broad support was expressed for the objective of streamlining UNCITRAL omnibus resolutions and for the consultative process, and appreciation was expressed to Panama for leading the process and to the secretariat for the progress made. As to the way forward, there was a suggestion to tentatively adopt the proposed guiding principles with changes, if necessary, and proceed to implementing some of the guiding principles incrementally with the engagement of Austria (the coordinator of UNCITRAL omnibus resolutions), UNCITRAL focal points of other States and the secretariat. That proposal received general support. In that connection, it was mentioned that once efforts were made to implement guiding principles those efforts were likely to sustain streamlined UNCITRAL omnibus resolutions for the foreseeable future.

304. Concerns were nonetheless expressed about some of the proposed guiding principles, such as the principle on the time limit regarding references to past events and the principle providing the rule of law as an example of a specific topic to which reference was made excessively. With regard to references to past events, although a suggestion was made to put them in an annex to the resolution, it was felt that it would be preferable to develop guidelines with sufficient flexibility. It was also underscored that as the process continued, it should be based on consensus and conducted in Vienna.

305. After discussion, the Commission requested the secretariat to continue to facilitate an open and flexible intersessional consultative process led in Vienna among States Members of the United Nations, involving not only delegates of Vienna-based Permanent Missions but also UNCITRAL focal points of member and observer States, with a view to preparing an UNCITRAL omnibus resolution reflecting some of the

[67] Ibid., *Seventy-eight Session, Supplement No. 17* (A/78/17), paras. 307–310.

[68] Ibid., para. 308.

guiding principles in 2024. In doing so, the Commission recommended the following flexible and tentative guiding principles that could be taken into account incrementally in preparing UNCITRAL omnibus resolutions: (a) limiting references to past events and decisions to a reasonable number of years prior to the date of the resolution to be adopted; (b) limiting references to one or two operative paragraphs addressing each thematic topic of the work of UNCITRAL; (c) shortening the length of paragraphs and consolidating them where appropriate; (d) giving preference to action-oriented language in operative paragraphs; (e) deleting preambular paragraphs and operative paragraphs that did not contain necessary basic information or recent updates on the work of UNCITRAL; (f) reorganizing and clustering information, ensuring coherence and avoiding repetition; and (g) inserting thematic headings where appropriate. The Commission encouraged States Members of the United Nations to continue to take part in the process and requested the secretariat to report on the progress made at its next session, in 2025.

XIII. Coordination and cooperation

A. General

306. The Commission had before it a note by the Secretariat (A/CN.9/1176) providing information on the activities of international organizations in the field of international trade law in which the secretariat had participated between the fifty-sixth session of the Commission and January 2024. The Commission noted that from 2025 onwards, reporting on coordination and cooperation activities would cover the full preceding calendar year. The Commission thanked the secretariat for its efforts to closely follow the work of other organizations and to cooperate and coordinate with them in the implementation of its own and those other organizations' work programmes, in particular UNIDROIT and HCCH.

307. The Commission noted with appreciation the cooperation between its secretariat and UNIDROIT in the preparation of the Model Law on Warehouse Receipts, which had been transmitted to the Commission for finalization and adoption during the present session. The Commission also noted the cooperation on various other UNIDROIT projects, including the legal nature of voluntary carbon credits, digital assets and private law, bank insolvency, international investment contracts, the legal structure of agricultural enterprises and best practices for effective enforcement. With regard to HCCH, the Commission noted that the UNCITRAL secretariat had continued its exchanges with the HCCH Permanent Bureau, focusing in particular on topics on their respective work programmes related to the digital economy, applicable law in insolvency proceedings and asset tracing and recovery.

308. More generally, the Commission expressed its satisfaction for the efforts made by the secretariat to cooperate and coordinate work with other organizations and entities, within and outside the United Nations system, both at a general level and on specific topics of the Commission's work programme, including the Economic Commission for Europe, the Economic and Monetary Community of Central Africa, the Economic and Social Commission for Asia and the Pacific, the Global Legal Entity Identifier Foundation, the Inter-Agency Task Force on Financing for Development, the International Bar Association, the International Centre for Settlement of Investment Disputes, the International Chamber of Commerce, the International Federation of Consulting Engineers, OECD, PCA, the Committee of Experts on Business and Trade Statistics, the United Nations Centre for Trade Facilitation and Electronic Business, UNCTAD, the United Nations Framework Convention on Climate Change secretariat, the United Nations Statistics Division, the World Bank Group, the World Intellectual Property Organization and the World Trade Organization.

309. The Commission heard that an event jointly organized by the Eurasian Economic Commission and the Russian Federation had been held on 20 June 2024 to promote the publication *COVID-19 and International Trade Law Instruments: a Legal Toolkit*

by the UNCITRAL Secretariat, prepared by the secretariat in order to mitigate the negative consequences of crises affecting international trade. The Commission expressed its appreciation to the secretariat for its contribution to that event, noted the usefulness of the toolkit for strengthening and promoting the development of an effective legal framework for preventing potential emergencies, and encouraged further activities to disseminate the toolkit and raise awareness about its contents among various stakeholders, including regional organizations and their member States.

310. The Commission reiterated the importance of coordinating the activities of organizations active in the field of international trade law, which was a core element of the mandate that UNCITRAL had received from the General Assembly,[69] as a means of avoiding duplication of efforts and promoting efficiency, consistency and coherence in the unification and harmonization of international trade law. The Commission noted instances in which the secretariats of UNCITRAL, UNIDROIT and HCCH had faced difficulties in coordinating their work. The Commission also noted the difficulties faced by member States in following various initiatives and the risk of scheduling conflicts among meetings of different organizations. The Commission welcomed the commitment of the secretariats to continue working closely to achieve greater coordination and to engage in closer cooperative dialogue in establishing their respective work programmes, agendas, dates of meetings and timelines in order to ensure efficient use of the resources of member States. The Commission was informed that the tripartite coordination meeting of UNCITRAL, UNIDROIT and HCCH had been held in April 2024 and that details would be reported to the Commission at its next session, in 2025.

B. Reports of other international organizations

311. The Commission took note of the statements made on behalf of international and regional organizations invited to the session, which focused on activities of relevance to UNCITRAL.

1. Asian-African Legal Consultative Organization

312. The Commission heard a statement by AALCO noting in particular that:

(a) AALCO regularly discussed the work of UNCITRAL at its annual sessions and strongly supported the response of UNCITRAL to new challenges;

(b) The AALCO secretariat had prepared a report on the work of UNCITRAL encouraging AALCO members to use key legislative instruments implemented by UNCITRAL (e.g. the Mauritius Convention,[70] the Singapore Convention on Mediation[71] and the United Nations Convention on the International Effects of Judicial Sales of Ships (the Beijing Convention on the Judicial Sale of Ships));[72]

(c) The work of UNCITRAL currently under way within Working Group III had been the focus of deliberations by AALCO member States at its annual sessions since 2018. AALCO member States would meet in Bangkok for the sixty-second annual session to deliberate in particular on issues relating to investor-State dispute settlement reform;

(d) The recent signing of the cooperation agreement between UNCITRAL and AALCO further evidenced their close working relationship.

[69] See General Assembly resolution 2205 (XXI), sect. II, para. 8.

[70] United Nations, *Treaty Series*, vol. 3208.

[71] *Official Records of the General Assembly, Seventy-third Session, Supplement No. 17* (A/73/17), annex I.

[72] General Assembly resolution 77/100, annex.

2. Organization for the Harmonization of Business Law in Africa

313. A representative of the secretariat read a statement on behalf of OHADA highlighting the following points:

(a) The common features of the mandates of UNCITRAL and OHADA related to the progressive harmonization and modernization of international trade law, and the frequent use of UNCITRAL texts (e.g. the United Nations Sales Convention (1980),[73] the UNCITRAL Model Law on Cross-Border Insolvency,[74] the *UNCITRAL Legislative Guide on Insolvency Law*,[75] the UNCITRAL Model Law on International Commercial Mediation and International Settlement Agreements Resulting from Mediation[76] and the UNCITRAL Model Law on International Commercial Arbitration (1985)[77]) by OHADA for its uniform acts on general commercial law, the organization of collective procedures for the discharge of liabilities, mediation and arbitration;

(b) The specificities of the legal integration undertaken by OHADA through the adoption of legal texts of direct application among its 17 member States and the establishment of a judicial body in charge of ensuring a consistent interpretation of OHADA law (the Common Court of Justice and Arbitration);

(c) The long-standing and forward-looking cooperation between both organizations, facilitated by the memorandum of understanding signed on 26 October 2016, and the interest of OHADA in the work of UNCITRAL on investor-State dispute settlement reform, as well as potential future work of OHADA on electronic transactions that could benefit from input by UNCITRAL.

3. Permanent Court of Arbitration

314. The representative of PCA made a statement providing an overview of the experience of PCA in 2023 with UNCITRAL instruments and addressing its cooperation with Working Groups II and III. The Commission was informed of the experience of PCA in providing registry support for international arbitration conducted under the UNCITRAL Arbitration Rules (including the 1976, 2010, 2013 and 2021 versions) and the role of the Secretary-General of PCA as designating authority or appointing authority under those Rules (including the review of arbitrator fees). The Commission noted that the UNCITRAL Rules on Transparency in Treaty-based Investor-State Arbitration[78] were applicable in two investor-State cases registered with PCA in 2023. The Commission noted with satisfaction the contributions made by PCA to the work of Working Groups II and III.

315. The Commission further noted that in August 2023, the General Assembly had adopted resolution 77/322 on the commemoration of the 125th anniversary of PCA, in which the Assembly had recognized, inter alia, the support provided by PCA and its participation in the work of various organizations of the United Nations system, including UNCITRAL.

4. UNIDROIT

316. The Secretary-General of UNIDROIT reported on developments concerning several UNIDROIT activities. The Commission was informed, in particular, about the following:

(a) The UNIDROIT secretariat had continued its excellent cooperation with UNCITRAL in the development of the draft UNCITRAL-UNIDROIT model law on warehouse receipts. The Model Law would not only be the first joint uniform law

---

[73] United Nations, Treaty Series, vol. 1489, No. 25567, p. 3.

[74] General Assembly resolution 52/158, annex.

[75] United Nations publication, Sales No. E.05.V.10.

[76] *Official Records of the General Assembly, Seventy-third Session, Supplement No. 17* (A/73/17), annex II.

[77] Ibid., *Fortieth Session, Supplement No. 17* (A/40/17), annex I.

[78] Ibid., *Sixty-eighth Session, Supplement No. 17* (A/68/17), annex I.

instrument adopted by UNCITRAL and UNIDROIT but also represented a significant addition to existing global legislative guidance texts for States to improve access to credit for small businesses, particularly in the agricultural sector;

(b) The UNIDROIT Governing Council and the General Assembly had approved the proposal to develop an international instrument on the legal nature of verified carbon credits in 2023. In 2024, the UNIDROIT Governing Council had expressed a positive opinion on the publication of the joint UNCITRAL-UNIDROIT study on the legal nature of verified carbon credits issued by independent carbon standard setters, prepared by both secretariats and discussed at the Joint Meeting of the UNCITRAL Expert Group and the UNIDROIT Working Group on the Legal Nature of Voluntary Carbon Credits (Vienna, 31 January and 1 February 2024);

(c) The UNIDROIT Working Group on Bank Insolvency had greatly benefited from the consideration of UNCITRAL instruments on insolvency and the UNCITRAL secretariat's participation as an observer;

(d) The UNIDROIT Working Group on Best Practices for Effective Enforcement had also benefited from the participation of the UNCITRAL secretariat. The project being carried out by the Working Group was considered relevant and complementary to ongoing work within UNCITRAL Working Group V on asset tracing and recovery in insolvency proceedings and to UNCITRAL texts on secured transactions;

(e) The UNCITRAL secretariat had also been active as an institutional observer in the UNIDROIT Project on Collaborative Legal Structures for Agricultural Enterprises and the UNIDROIT Working Group on International Investment Contracts;

(f) UNIDROIT had continued to work closely with the UNCITRAL secretariat as partners of the Joint Network for Coordinating and Supporting Secured Transactions Reforms.

C. International governmental and non-governmental organizations invited to sessions of UNCITRAL and its working groups

317. The Commission recalled that, at its fiftieth session, in 2017, it had requested the secretariat to provide information about intergovernmental organizations and non-governmental organizations invited to sessions of UNCITRAL in writing for future sessions.[79] At its fifty-seventh session, the Commission had before it a note by the Secretariat submitted pursuant to that request (A/CN.9/1187). The note presented information, as at 15 May 2024, about the newly accepted non-governmental organizations, as well as the non-governmental organizations whose applications had been declined, since the issuance of the last note by the Secretariat on that topic (A/CN.9/1142).

318. The Commission took note of that information, as well as of the separate list of additional non-governmental organizations invited only to the sessions of Working Group III while it was working on issues relating to investor-State dispute settlement reform.

XIV. Non-legislative activities

A. General

319. With reference to the notes by the Secretariat (A/CN.9/1174 and the addenda thereto), the Commission expressed its appreciation to the secretariat for delivering the reported activities and planning future activities and to all relevant stakeholders for supporting them. Those activities were considered essential for disseminating

[79] Ibid., *Seventy-second Session, Supplement No. 17* (A/72/17), para. 364.

knowledge about the Commission's texts and ongoing work and increasing understanding and uptake of them.

320. The Commission welcomed, in particular, the milestones reached in the implementation of formal agreements with the Ministry of Commerce of China; the Department of Justice of the government of Hong Kong, China; the Ministry of Justice of the Republic of Korea and Incheon Metropolitan City; the Ministry of Commerce and the National Competitiveness Center of Saudi Arabia; the Government of Singapore; and the Ministry of Foreign Affairs of Viet Nam. It also welcomed the increased number and variety of cooperation frameworks put in place between the secretariat, including the UNCITRAL Regional Centre for Asia and the Pacific and international, regional and national organizations and institutions, and the results achieved so far under those cooperation frameworks, such as the expansion of the 2023 UNCITRAL Days in Africa, the Arab States, Asia and the Pacific, and Latin America and the Caribbean.[80]

321. The Commission noted with appreciation the secretariat's diligence in providing full and detailed information about its non-legislative activities and their funding. Given the expanding reach and intensity of those activities, the Commission encouraged the secretariat to explore a more concise way of presenting them.

B. Technical cooperation and assistance activities by the UNCITRAL secretariat based in Vienna

322. With reference to the technical cooperation and assistance activities reported in document A/CN.9/1174/Add.1/Rev.1, the Commission noted that those activities had been led by the UNCITRAL secretariat based in Vienna, often with the support of the UNCITRAL Regional Centre for Asia and the Pacific where applicable, and had been aimed at either: (a) raising awareness of UNCITRAL texts, building capacity to use them and otherwise promoting their adoption and increased understanding and effective use of them (such as through training activities for judges and legal practitioners); or (b) providing advice and assistance to States on the adoption and use of UNCITRAL texts (such as through a review of draft legislation).

323. The Commission noted the significant increase in the number of those activities across all thematic areas during the reporting period and efforts to ensure their enhanced and continuous impact. It welcomed, in particular, the secretariat's plans to prepare a multilingual curriculum for training judges and insolvency practitioners on the basis of the UNCITRAL cross-border insolvency framework, and also noted in that context the secretariat's plans to update the *UNCITRAL Practice Guide on Cross-Border Insolvency Cooperation*[81] discussed under a different agenda item during the session (see para. 256 above).

C. Technical cooperation and assistance activities by the UNCITRAL Regional Centre for Asia and the Pacific

324. With reference to the report on activities of the UNCITRAL Regional Centre for Asia and the Pacific in document A/CN.9/1174/Add.2, the Commission welcomed a statement by the Philippines commending the work of the Regional Centre and a statement by the Republic of Korea expressing its continued support and inviting other delegations to participate in the various in-person and hybrid activities spearheaded by the Regional Centre to promote legal certainty in international commercial transactions in Asia and the Pacific. The Commission recognized the important benefits for the Asia and Pacific region of the Regional Centre, which had continued to enhance levels of awareness, adoption and implementation of UNCITRAL texts in

[80] See unofficial reports of the 2023 UNCITRAL Days at https://uncitral.un.org/en/commission.
[81] United Nations publication, Sales No. E.10.V.6. Available at https://uncitral.un.org/en/texts/insolvency/explanatorytexts/practice_guide_cross-border_insolvency.

the region. In particular, the Commission commended the active engagement by the Regional Centre with least developed countries, landlocked developing countries and small island developing States of the region, with 18 such jurisdictions co-hosting or participating in activities carried out by the Regional Centre.

325. The Commission also commended the Regional Centre for co-organizing a record number of activities, including in-person flagship activities, while continuing to expand the reach and accessibility of all activities through online or hybrid means, resulting in broader stakeholder engagement. Those activities included the tenth edition of the UNCITRAL Asia-Pacific Days, in which 17 events were co-hosted with 32 partnering universities and institutions across 11 jurisdictions in the region and which, as in previous years, had proved highly successful in support of the activities and objectives of the Regional Centre.[82]

326. The Commission noted that the Regional Centre was staffed with one professional-level staff member, one programme assistant, one team assistant and two legal experts secondees; that its core project budget allowed for the occasional employment of experts and consultants; and that, during the reporting period, the Regional Centre had received 17 interns. The Commission also noted that the Regional Centre relied on the annual financial contribution from the Incheon Metropolitan City to the trust fund for UNCITRAL symposiums for its operation.

327. The Commission expressed its gratitude to the Incheon Metropolitan City for its generous contribution to that trust fund ($500,000 from 2011 to 2016 and $450,000 from 2017 to 2026), which allowed the Regional Centre to meet the cost of its operation and programme. The Commission also expressed its gratitude to the Ministry of Justice of the Republic of Korea and to the government of Hong Kong, China, for the extension of their contribution of two legal experts on non-reimbursable loans. The Commission reiterated its call to relevant stakeholders to provide additional resources and other support to the Regional Centre.

328. The Commission expressed strong support for the Regional Centre's continued coordination and cooperation efforts with regional stakeholders, development banks and other institutions active in trade law reform, and with United Nations funds, programmes and specialized agencies active in the region. It reiterated its request to the Regional Centre to continue its efforts to raise additional resources and support for its activities.

D. Ensuring a uniform interpretation and application of international conventions and uniform laws in the field of the law of international trade (CLOUT, digests and related activities)

329. With reference to document A/CN.9/1174/Add.3, which provided information on the system for the collection and dissemination of information on court decisions and arbitral awards relating to UNCITRAL texts (known as "Case Law on UNCITRAL Texts" (CLOUT)), digests of case law and other related activities, the Commission reiterated its belief that CLOUT continued to be relevant for promoting a uniform interpretation and application of UNCITRAL texts across jurisdictions. It noted with satisfaction the progress achieved with CLOUT in the second half of 2023, despite difficulties that the secretariat had faced with its operation owing to the United Nations liquidity crisis. It noted in particular: (a) the number of CLOUT abstracts published; (b) coordination achieved between CLOUT and the 1958 New York Convention website (www.newyorkconvention1958.org); and (c) other outreach activities undertaken that, inter alia, resulted in an increased number of users of the CLOUT database.

[82] See https://uncitral.un.org/sites/uncitral.un.org/files/media-documents/uncitral/en/2024_ap_day_report.pdf (unofficial document, only in English).

330. The Commission reaffirmed the role of national correspondents as the backbone of CLOUT. Acknowledging the need for national correspondents to come from a wider range of States, the Commission called on all States that had not yet designated national correspondents to do so, ensuring gender balance in their designations.

331. The Commission noted that during the reporting period, a high number of published abstracts had been prepared by the secretariat and voluntary contributors, rather than by national correspondents. The Commission called on all States that had designated national correspondents to encourage them to fulfil their role, with the assistance of the secretariat if necessary. The Commission acknowledged that the timely identification of relevant case law and good quality CLOUT abstracts were key to the continued relevance and effectiveness of CLOUT.

332. The Commission recalled the establishment of a CLOUT steering committee comprising one representative appointed by each State.[83] It invited States that had not yet designated a steering committee member to do so, noting the need to ensure the geographical and gender balanced composition of that committee.

333. The Commission welcomed arrangements made by the secretariat to update the *UNCITRAL Digest of Case Law on the Model Law on International Commercial Arbitration*[84] and prepare an analytical compilation of case law on the 1974 Limitation Convention.[85] The Commission encouraged national correspondents and other relevant stakeholders to bring case law that was related to that Convention but that had not yet been published in CLOUT to the attention of the secretariat. The Commission authorized the secretariat to publish the updated edition of the *UNCITRAL Digest of Case Law on the Model Law on International Commercial Arbitration* and the analytical compilation of case law on the 1974 Limitation Convention, including electronically, in the six official languages of the United Nations, and to make them generally known and available.

334. The Commission also authorized the secretariat to pursue its consultations with database and search engine platforms with a view to outsourcing the upgrading of the CLOUT database, subject to three main guiding principles: (a) access must remain free of charge; (b) UNCITRAL must keep the intellectual property rights to the CLOUT abstracts made available; and (c) the CLOUT abstracts must be made available in the six official languages of the United Nations.

E. Operation of the transparency repository under article 8 of the UNCITRAL Rules on Transparency in Treaty-based Investor-State Arbitration

335. The Commission recalled that article 8 of the UNCITRAL Rules on Transparency in Treaty-based Investor-State Arbitration[86] (the Rules on Transparency) envisaged the establishment of a repository of published information (the transparency repository).[87] The Commission further recalled, with reference to information provided in document A/CN.9/1174/Add.4, that the UNCITRAL secretariat had operated the transparency repository initially as a pilot project until the end of 2016, and thereafter as a project from 2016 until 2024, both phases funded entirely by voluntary contributions. The Commission reiterated its appreciation to the European Union, the Fund for International Development of the Organization of the Petroleum Exporting Countries and the Federal Ministry for Economic Cooperation and

[83] *Official Records of the General Assembly, Seventy-fourth Session, Supplement No. 17* (A/74/17), para. 244.

[84] United Nations publication, Sales No. E.12.V.9. Available at https://uncitral.un.org/sites/uncitral.un.org/files/media-documents/uncitral/en/mal-digest-2012-e.pdf.

[85] United Nations, *Treaty Series*, vol. 1511, No. 26119, p. 3.

[86] *Official Records of the General Assembly, Sixty-eighth Session, Supplement No. 17* (A/68/17), annex I.

[87] See the Rules on Transparency, art. 8.

Development (BMZ) of Germany for their voluntary contributions, which had made it possible for the secretariat to operate the transparency repository as a central feature of both the Rules on Transparency and the Mauritius Convention[88] (together referred to as the "UNCITRAL transparency standards"), providing a consolidated, transparent and easily accessible global case record database for all investor-State arbitrations conducted under the UNCITRAL transparency standards.[89]

336. The Commission noted that new cases were added to the transparency repository on a regular basis and that the UNCITRAL transparency standards were promoted by a legal officer in the UNCITRAL secretariat responsible for managing and operating the transparency repository. The Commission expressed its appreciation for those activities and for the activities planned throughout 2024 for the tenth anniversary of the UNCITRAL transparency standards. Recalling information provided on the uptake by States of the Rules on Transparency in a separate note by the Secretariat before the Commission at the current session (A/CN.9/1172/Rev.1, paras. 16 and 17), the Commission noted with interest the tendency towards greater transparency in treaty-based investor-State dispute settlement. It expressed support for the continued operation of the transparency repository as a key mechanism for promoting transparency in investor-State arbitration.

337. The Commission recalled that the General Assembly had requested the Secretary-General to continue to operate the transparency repository, through the secretariat of the Commission, and requested the Secretary-General to keep the General Assembly informed of developments regarding the funding and budgetary situation of the transparency repository.[90] The Commission noted that the transparency repository would continue to operate through August 2024, funded entirely by voluntary contributions from the European Union and the Federal Ministry for Economic Cooperation and Development of Germany. With respect to the funding of the project beyond August 2024, the Commission was informed that the secretariat was in contact with interested States and intergovernmental organizations and that the European Union had expressed an interest in continuing to provide funding for the project until the end of 2027.[91]

338. In the light of those developments and with reference to the various options for the future operation of the transparency repository set out in paragraph 10 of document A/CN.9/1174/Add.4, the Commission decided to recommend to the General Assembly that it request the Secretary-General to continue to operate, through the secretariat of the Commission, the transparency repository in accordance with article 8 of the Rules on Transparency as a continuation of the project until the end of 2027, subject to funding. The Commission noted that the UNCITRAL secretariat should continue to keep the General Assembly and the Commission informed of developments regarding the funding and budgetary situation of the transparency repository based on its operation. The Commission reiterated its appeal to all States, international organizations and other interested entities to consider making contributions towards the operation of the transparency repository, and to make them, if possible, in the form of multi-year contributions, so as to facilitate planning.

F. Online and social media presence of UNCITRAL

339. With reference to document A/CN.9/1174/Add.5, reiterating the significance of the UNCITRAL website as a multilingual source of information on international trade law, the Commission welcomed the statistics on the usage of that website. It also welcomed the statistics and highlights related to the usage of UNCITRAL social media channels, including the fact that, by providing additional information about the work of the Commission, those channels generated more interest in that work. The

[88] United Nations, *Treaty Series*, vol. 3208.
[89] General Assembly resolution 70/115, para. 2.
[90] See, most recently, General Assembly resolution 78/103, para. 4.
[91] See A/CN.9/1174/Add.4, footnote 14.

Commission encouraged efforts to enhance the impact of the UNCITRAL website and social media presence on the dissemination of information about modern legal developments, including case law, in the field of international trade law, in compliance with applicable United Nations rules and regulations, including with regard to accessibility.

340. The Commission commended the continuing development and expansion of the UNCITRAL e-learning programme. It welcomed efforts to make all UNCITRAL e-learning courses available in the six official languages of the United Nations and appealed for voluntary contributions to the trust fund for UNCITRAL symposiums to that end. It expressed its appreciation to China for funding the development of the courses and their translation into Chinese, and to the European Bank for Reconstruction and Development for providing funding for the translation of the e-learning course on public procurement and public-private partnerships into Arabic and Russian.

341. Acknowledging the increased demand for, and resource-intensive task of, keeping the Commission's online presence up to date, the Commission encouraged the use of innovative approaches to achieve that goal. The Commission encouraged the secretariat to explore different social media platforms to raise awareness of the work of UNCITRAL among younger generations.

G. UNCITRAL Law Library, publications, press releases and other outreach activities

342. With reference to document A/CN.9/1174/Add.6, the Commission emphasized the importance of the UNCITRAL Law Library, the reported outreach activities, timely responses by the Library's staff to information requests, including online, and the continued maintenance and development of the UNCITRAL bibliography.

343. The Commission reiterated its request to States and other relevant stakeholders, such as organizations active in international commercial law reform, to advise the secretariat when legislation implementing an UNCITRAL model law or other relevant text had been enacted. That information was considered relevant not only for accurately reporting the status of UNCITRAL texts (see chapter XV of the present report on the status of conventions, model laws and other legal texts emanating from the work of UNCITRAL, as well as the Convention on the Recognition and Enforcement of Foreign Arbitral Awards) but also for collecting and disseminating information on national legislation in the field of international trade law, including through the UNCITRAL Law Library, press releases and other outreach activities of the UNCITRAL secretariat. The Commission also appealed to publishers, especially those representing or affiliated with organizations invited to UNCITRAL sessions, to donate to the UNCITRAL Law Library their books, periodicals and other materials related to the work of UNCITRAL or international commercial law or, where donation was not possible, to grant a discounted rate for such materials. The Commission expressed its appreciation to those publishers that had already done so.

344. The Commission noted the plans of the secretariat to update *A Guide to UNCITRAL: Basic Facts about the United Nations Commission on International Trade Law*[92] for the upcoming sixtieth anniversary of the establishment of UNCITRAL. The Commission authorized the secretariat to publish the updated guide, including electronically, in the six official languages of the United Nations and to make it generally known and available.

345. The Commission invited the secretariat to consider means and implications of providing access to materials in the UNCITRAL Law Library to delegates outside Vienna.

---

[92] Available at https://uncitral.un.org/sites/uncitral.un.org/files/media-documents/uncitral/en/12-57491-guide-to-uncitral-e.pdf.

H. Internship programme and moot competitions

346. With reference to the information provided in paragraphs 1 to 4 of document A/CN.9/1174/Add.7, the Commission welcomed the continuation of the UNCITRAL internship programme at its secretariat in Vienna and at the UNCITRAL Regional Centre for Asia and the Pacific, including remote internships that helped to broaden the access of eligible candidates from underrepresented States to the internship programme and to enhance linguistic and geographical diversity.

347. With reference to the information provided in paragraphs 5–17 of document A/CN.9/1174/Add.7, the Commission commended the secretariat for its continued co-sponsorship of major international commercial law moot competitions, such as the Willem C. Vis International Commercial Arbitration Moot and the Ian Fletcher International Insolvency Law Moot, and the continued expansion of such moot competitions in different languages.

348. The Commission noted that, together with the annual UNCITRAL Days held by the UNCITRAL secretariat in different regions (see para. 320 above), internships at the UNCITRAL secretariat and international commercial law moot competitions were a means of reaching out to more law students and young academics and professionals in developing countries for the purpose of providing them with training on UNCITRAL-related subjects. The Commission welcomed the efforts of all concerned to diversify geographical and gender representation in those activities and address the special needs of developing countries in building the professional cadre in international commercial law. The Commission reiterated its call to States and other relevant stakeholders to bring information about internship opportunities at the UNCITRAL secretariat, international commercial law moot competitions and UNCITRAL Days to the attention of interested persons and to consider providing financial support to interested eligible and qualified candidates to enable them to participate in those activities.

I. Planned activities

349. The Commission expressed its appreciation to the secretariat for the information in document A/CN.9/1174/Add.8 about other planned non-legislative activities. The Commission noted that those activities included, in addition to regular annual and biennial events, new events, including on the newly adopted texts of UNCITRAL.

350. The Commission noted that giving advance notice about upcoming non-legislative activities had multiple benefits, allowing States and other stakeholders to plan for such activities and ensure meaningful engagement.

J. Resources and funding

351. With reference to the information in document A/CN.9/1174/Add.9 about resources and funding available to the UNCITRAL secretariat for its non-legislative activities in 2023,[93] the Commission expressed its appreciation for the contributions made to the trust fund for UNCITRAL symposiums and renewed its appeal to Governments, relevant bodies of the United Nations system, organizations, institutions and individuals to make voluntary contributions to that trust fund, in particular in the

[93] For completeness, document A/CN.9/1174/Add.9 lists contributions made to the trust fund for UNCITRAL symposiums for other purposes (such as to finance the participation of developing countries in sessions of Working Group III (Investor-State Dispute Settlement Reform)). It also lists a contribution made to the trust fund established to provide travel assistance to developing countries that are members of UNCITRAL. A contribution made in 2023 to the trust fund for UNCITRAL symposiums to support the stocktaking of developments in dispute resolution in the digital economy was reported to the Commission separately, in document A/CN.9/1189 (see para. 278 above).

form of multi-year contributions that would enhance the secretariat's ability to plan non-legislative activities in order to meet the increased demand for them and derive the benefits noted in the preceding sections. The Commission reiterated the importance of the United Nations Pledging Conference for Development Activities continuing to include both the trust fund for UNCITRAL symposiums and the trust fund established to provide travel assistance to developing countries that are members of UNCITRAL in its list of trust funds of relevance to the United Nations development system.

352. The Commission also renewed its call to all relevant stakeholders for the financing of special projects, such as the Regional Centre for Asia and the Pacific, the upgrade of the CLOUT database, the continued operation of the transparency repository and other needs noted in the preceding sections. The value of in-kind contributions, for example, to the CLOUT database and the UNCITRAL Law Library, as noted in the preceding sections, was also underscored.

XV. Status of conventions, model laws and other legal texts emanating from the work of UNCITRAL, as well as the Convention on the Recognition and Enforcement of Foreign Arbitral Awards

353. The Commission considered the status of the conventions and model laws emanating from its work, as well as the status of the Convention on the Recognition and Enforcement of Foreign Arbitral Awards (1958 New York Convention),[94] on the basis of a note by the Secretariat (A/CN.9/1172/Rev.1). The Commission noted with appreciation the information on treaty actions and legislative enactments received since its fifty-sixth session.

354. The Commission also noted the following actions and legislative enactments[95] made known to the UNCITRAL secretariat subsequent to the submission of the above-mentioned note:

(a) UNCITRAL Model Law on International Commercial Arbitration (1985)[96] as amended in 2006.[97] Legislation based on the Model Law has been adopted in 93 States in a total of 126 jurisdictions. New legislation based on the Model Law has been adopted in Azerbaijan (2024), Guyana (2024), Israel (2024) and Malawi (2024);

(b) Singapore Convention on Mediation (New York, 2018).[98] Signature by Iraq and ratification by Sri Lanka; 57 signatories; 14 States parties;

(c) UNCITRAL Model Law on Cross-Border Insolvency (1997).[99] Legislation based on the Model Law has been adopted in 60 States in a total of 63 jurisdictions. New legislation based on the Model Law has been adopted in Costa Rica (2021);

[94] United Nations, *Treaty Series*, vol. 330, No. 4739, p. 3.

[95] In calculating the number of States in which a model law has been adopted, the UNCITRAL secretariat counts all States where that model law has been enacted either at the national or subnational level. In calculating the number of jurisdictions in which a model law has been adopted, the secretariat counts all subnational jurisdictions that have enacted a model law, as well as States that have adopted it at the national level, but excludes States that have not adopted it at the national level. For example, if State A and State B have adopted a model law at the national level and in State C, two subnational jurisdictions have adopted a model law, then the records would indicate that the model law has been adopted in three States in a total of four jurisdictions (i.e. State C would not be counted as a jurisdiction, only as a State).

[96] *Official Records of the General Assembly, Fortieth Session, Supplement No. 17* (A/40/17), annex I.

[97] Ibid., *Sixty-first Session, Supplement No. 17* (A/61/17), annex I.

[98] Ibid., *Seventy-third Session, Supplement No. 17* (A/73/17), annex I.

[99] General Assembly resolution 52/158, annex.

(d) Beijing Convention on the Judicial Sale of Ships (New York, 2022).[100] Signature by Belgium, Luxembourg and the European Union, ratification by El Salvador; 20 signatories, 1 State party;

(e) Electronic Communications Convention (New York, 2005).[101] Domestic legislation enacting the substantive provisions of the Convention has been adopted in 44 States. New domestic legislation based on the Convention has been adopted in Timor-Leste (2024);

(f) UNCITRAL Model Law on Electronic Commerce (1996).[102] Legislation based on or influenced by the Model Law has been adopted in 87 States in a total of 170 jurisdictions. New legislation based on the Model Law has been adopted in Timor-Leste (2024);

(g) UNCITRAL Model Law on Electronic Signatures (2001).[103] Legislation based on or influenced by the Model Law has been adopted in 40 States in a total of 42 jurisdictions. New legislation based on the Model Law has been adopted in Timor-Leste (2024);

(h) Model Law on Electronic Transferable Records (2017).[104] Legislation based on or influenced by the Model Law has been adopted in nine States in a total of nine jurisdictions. New legislation based on the Model Law has been adopted in Timor-Leste (2024).

355. The Commission expressed appreciation to the General Assembly for the support it provided to UNCITRAL in its activities and in performing its distinct role in furthering the dissemination of international commercial law. In particular, the Commission referred to the long-established practice of the General Assembly, upon acting on UNCITRAL texts, to recommend to States to give favourable consideration to UNCITRAL texts and to request the Secretary-General to publish UNCITRAL texts, including electronically, in the six official languages of the United Nations, and take other measures to disseminate UNCITRAL texts as broadly as possible to Governments and all other relevant stakeholders. The Commission recalled that in that context, the General Assembly requested States and other relevant stakeholders, such as organizations active in international commercial law reform, to advise the secretariat when legislation implementing an UNCITRAL model law or other relevant texts had been enacted. The Commission considered it important for States and other stakeholders to do so in order to ensure accurate reporting by the secretariat of the status of UNCITRAL texts.

XVI. Bibliography of recent writings related to the work of UNCITRAL

356. Considering the broader impact of UNCITRAL texts, the Commission took note of the bibliography of recent writings related to the work of UNCITRAL (A/CN.9/1171) and the influence of UNCITRAL texts as described in academic and professional literature. The Commission noted, in particular, that the consolidated bibliography contained more than 12,405 entries, reproduced in English and in the original language versions. The Commission further noted the importance of facilitating a comprehensive approach to the creation of the bibliography and the need to remain informed of activities of non-governmental organizations active in the field of international trade law. In that regard, the Commission recalled and repeated its request that non-governmental organizations invited to the Commission's annual

[100] General Assembly resolution 77/100, annex. The Convention has not yet entered into force; it requires three States parties for entry into force.
[101] General Assembly resolution 60/21, annex.
[102] General Assembly resolution 51/162, annex.
[103] General Assembly resolution 56/80, annex.
[104] *Official Records of the General Assembly, Seventy-second Session, Supplement No. 17* (A/72/17), annex I.

session donate copies of their journals, reports and other publications to the UNCITRAL Law Library for review.[105] The Commission expressed its appreciation to all non-governmental organizations that had donated materials.

XVII. Current role of UNCITRAL in promoting the rule of law

A. Introduction

357. The Commission recalled that the item had been on its agenda since its forty-first session, in 2008,[106] in response to the General Assembly's invitation to the Commission to comment, in its report to the General Assembly, on the Commission's current role in promoting the rule of law.[107] The Commission further recalled that, at its forty-first to fifty-sixth sessions, from 2008 to 2023, the Commission, in its annual reports to the General Assembly,[108] had transmitted comments on its role in promoting the rule of law at the national and international levels.

358. At the current session, the Commission had before it a note by the Secretariat on the role of UNCITRAL in promoting the rule of law at the national and international levels (A/CN.9/1177). The Commission noted that the General Assembly, in paragraph 21 of its resolution 78/112, had reiterated its invitation to the Commission to comment on its current role in promoting the rule of law (for the transmitted comments, see sect. B below). The Commission noted that in paragraph 24 of the same resolution, the General Assembly had invited Member States, under the agenda item entitled "The rule of law at the national and international levels", to focus their comments during the upcoming Sixth Committee debate on the subtopic, "The full, equal and equitable participation at all levels in the international legal system".

359. The Commission highlighted the relevance of its work to the promotion of the rule of law and the implementation of the Sustainable Development Goals. The Commission reiterated its request to States, the secretariat, organizations and institutions to continue their efforts to increase awareness of the role of UNCITRAL standards and activities in promoting the rule of law at the national and international levels and of their contribution to the implementation of the Sustainable Development Goals.

[105] Ibid., *Supplement No. 17* (A/70/17), para. 264. See also para. 343 above.

[106] For the decision of the Commission to include the item on its agenda, see *Official Records of the General Assembly, Sixty-second Session, Supplement No. 17* (A/62/17), part two, paras. 111–113.

[107] General Assembly resolutions 62/70, para. 3; 63/128, para. 7; 64/116, para. 9; 65/32, para. 10; 66/102, para. 12; 67/97, para. 14; 68/116, para. 14; 69/123, para. 17; 70/118, para. 20; 71/148, para. 22; 72/119, para. 25; 73/207, para. 20; 74/191, para. 20; 75/141, para. 20; 76/117, para. 20; 77/110, para. 20; and 78/112, para. 21.

[108] *Official Records of the General Assembly, Sixty-third Session, Supplement No. 17* and corrigendum (A/63/17 and Corr.1), para. 386; ibid., *Sixty-fourth Session, Supplement No. 17* (A/64/17), paras. 413–419; ibid., *Sixty-fifth Session, Supplement No. 17* (A/65/17), paras. 313–336; ibid., *Sixty-sixth Session, Supplement No. 17* (A/66/17), paras. 299–321; ibid., *Sixty-seventh Session, Supplement No. 17* (A/67/17), paras. 195–227; ibid., *Sixty-eighth Session, Supplement No. 17* (A/68/17), paras. 267–291; ibid., *Sixty-ninth Session, Supplement No. 17* (A/69/17), paras. 215–240; ibid., *Seventieth Session, Supplement No. 17* (A/70/17), paras. 318–324; ibid., *Seventy-first Session, Supplement No. 17* (A/71/17), paras. 317–342; ibid., *Seventy-second Session, Supplement No. 17* (A/72/17), paras. 435–441; ibid., *Seventy-third Session, Supplement No. 17* (A/73/17), paras. 232 and 233; ibid., *Seventy-fourth Session, Supplement No. 17* (A/74/17), paras. 303–308; *Seventy-fifth Session, Supplement No. 17* (A/75/17), para. 25; ibid., *Seventy-sixth Session, Supplement No. 17* (A/76/17), paras. 370–374; ibid., *Seventy-seventh Session, Supplement No. 17* (A/77/17), paras. 308–315; and ibid., *Seventy-eighth Session, Supplement No. 17* (A/78/17), paras. 299–304.

B. UNCITRAL comments to the General Assembly

360. In formulating its comments to the General Assembly in response to the invitation contained in paragraph 21 of General Assembly resolution 78/112, the Commission bore in mind the subtopic of the upcoming debates of the Sixth Committee on the rule of law, "The full, equal and equitable participation at all levels in the international legal system". The comments covered relevant discussions held at prior sessions of the Commission and described the relevance of the mandate of the Commission and its work methods to the subtopic.

361. The Commission recalled its consideration of issues relevant to that subtopic at its sessions in 2012,[109] 2015,[110] 2016,[111] and 2017.[112] At its forty-fifth session, in 2012, in its comments to the high-level meeting on the rule of law, the Commission had acknowledged the importance of participation in the international legal system at all levels when it had noted that local needs relating to commercial law reforms must be made known to the international community and that the international community needed to understand the importance of addressing those needs and, in the long run, building the local capacity of States to engage in law reforms.[113] At its forty-eighth session, in 2015, in comments made by the Commission on the role of its multilateral treaty processes in promoting and advancing the rule of law, the Commission had brought to the attention of the General Assembly issues relating to its treaty process that required attention, including the need to increase participation by all countries in the rule-formulating work of UNCITRAL and enhance the local capacity of States from various regions, with different legal systems and different levels of development, including least developed and small island developing countries.[114] At its forty-ninth session, in 2016, in its comments on the practices of States in the implementation of UNCITRAL treaties, it had noted that the quality of implementation of treaties emanating from the work of UNCITRAL often depended on the quality of treaty-making processes, including the level and quality of participation by States and other interested stakeholders in the rule-formulating work of UNCITRAL.[115] At its fiftieth session, in 2017, in comments made by the Commission on its current role in promoting the rule of law at the national and international levels, it recommended the further dissemination of the Guidance Note on Strengthening United Nations Support to States, Upon Their Request, to Implement Sound Commercial Law Reforms,[116] which provided guiding principles and a framework for strengthening United Nations support to States, upon their request, to implement commercial law reforms on the basis of internationally accepted standards.[117]

362. With regard to its mandate and work methods, the Commission highlighted how its ongoing work on the reform of investor-State dispute settlement, the continuing development of the CLOUT database, the study on the aspects of international trade law related to voluntary carbon credits, as well as its broader methods of work and composition, had contributed to the full, equal and equitable participation at all levels in the international legal system.

363. With regard to its work on the reform of investor-State dispute settlement, the Commission highlighted the efforts made to provide for full, equal and equitable

[109] *Official Records of the General Assembly, Sixty-seventh Session, Supplement No. 17* (A/67/17), paras. 218–223.

[110] Ibid., *Seventieth Session, Supplement No. 17* (A/70/17), paras. 318–324.

[111] Ibid., *Seventy-first Session, Supplement No. 17* (A/71/17), paras. 332–342.

[112] Ibid., *Seventy-second Session, Supplement No. 17* (A/72/17), para. 435–441.

[113] Ibid., *Sixty-seventh Session, Supplement No. 17* (A/67/17), paras. 218–223.

[114] Ibid., *Seventieth Session, Supplement No. 17* (A/70/17), paras. 318–324.

[115] Ibid., *Seventy-first Session, Supplement No. 17* (A/71/17), paras. 332–342.

[116] United Nations Commission on International Trade Law, "Guidance Note on Strengthening United Nations Support to States, Upon Their Request, to Implement Sound Commercial Law Reforms". Available at https://uncitral.un.org/sites/uncitral.un.org/files/englishguidance_note.pdf.

[117] *Official Records of the General Assembly, Seventy-second Session, Supplement No. 17* (A/72/17), paras. 435–441.

participation, both in respect of the expected outcomes of the reform of the investor-State dispute settlement system and the reform process itself. In terms of substantive outcomes, the Commission recalled that, at its current session, it had adopted in principle the Statute of the Advisory Centre on International Investment Dispute Resolution (see para. 167 above). It was recalled that the text focused on inclusivity in the international legal system by ensuring that the current system of investor-State dispute settlement regained legitimacy and that there were mechanisms for States, especially least developed and developing countries, to prevent, mitigate and defend themselves against foreign investors in international investment disputes. It was further recalled that the Advisory Centre on International Investment Dispute Resolution was aimed at providing training support and assistance in the area of international investment dispute resolution and enhancing the capacity of States to prevent and handle international investment disputes, in particular least developed countries and developing countries. It was also recalled that the Advisory Centre would provide representation and advisory services in international investment disputes.

364. With regard to process, the Commission recalled that the initial mandate for the investor-State dispute settlement reform project had stated that, in discharging the mandate, Working Group III would ensure that the deliberations would benefit from the widest possible breadth of available expertise from all stakeholders, be Government-led, with high-level input from all Governments, and be consensus-based and fully transparent.[118] In that context, it was recalled that participation in the work on investor-State dispute settlement reform had been increased through financial support provided by donors for travel and simultaneous interpretation at informal meetings.[119]

365. The Commission highlighted the inclusive nature of the CLOUT system and the related database, which provided access to case law in the six official languages of the United Nations and analysis of cases from relevant regions and served as a foundation for the promotion of the uniform interpretation and application of international commercial law standards. The Commission called for contributions from all legal traditions to the CLOUT database, which supported inclusive participation in the international legal system.[120]

366. The Commission also highlighted the inclusive character of its request to the secretariat to develop a detailed study on the aspects of international trade law related to voluntary carbon credits.[121] In its request, the Commission had asked the secretariat to consult with all Member States, to invite all Member States to nominate experts to provide input to the work of the secretariat in that area and to aim for as wide a representation as possible, in particular representation from developing countries.[122] To support those requests, a questionnaire on voluntary carbon credits had been circulated to all States Members of the United Nations, affording them an opportunity to provide their input and nominate experts.

367. Lastly, the Commission highlighted how its methods of work supported inclusivity in the international legal system, especially by broadening participation through remote participation in meetings. It was recalled that during the coronavirus disease (COVID-19) pandemic, remote participation in UNCITRAL meetings had been a necessity[123] but that although the global health emergency had ended, member States had expressed their desire to continue to have the possibility of participating

---

[118] Ibid., para. 264.

[119] Ibid., *Seventy-eighth Session, Supplement No. 17* (A/78/17), paras. 154 and 258.

[120] Ibid., para. 271.

[121] Ibid., para. 199.

[122] Ibid.

[123] Ibid., *Seventy-fifth Session, Supplement No. 17* (A/75/17), part one, para. 40; ibid., part two, paras. 1, 22; ibid., *Seventy-sixth Session, Supplement No. 17* (A/76/17), para. 25 (i); ibid., *Seventy-seventh Session, Supplement No. 17* (A/77/17), para. 237.

in UNCITRAL sessions remotely.[124] It was further recalled that, when agreeing to arrange for continued remote participation, the Commission had stressed that the arrangement should promote inclusivity and should seek to be effective in relation to costs and budgets.[125] However, it was noted that the provision of a streaming or videoconferencing platform for remote participation in meetings came at an added cost not included in the current budget and had been discontinued due to the current liquidity crisis at the United Nations.

368. The Commission also considered the expected contribution of its ongoing work on investor-State dispute settlement reform, asset tracing in insolvency proceedings, applicable law in insolvency proceedings, dispute resolution in the digital economy and negotiable cargo documents to the achievement of the Sustainable Development Goals.

XVIII. Relevant General Assembly resolutions

369. The Commission recalled that, at its fiftieth session, in 2017, it had requested the secretariat to replace an oral report to the Commission on relevant General Assembly resolutions with a written report to be issued before the session.[126] Pursuant to that request, the Commission had before it, at its current session, a note by the Secretariat (A/CN.9/1173) summarizing the content of the operative paragraphs of General Assembly resolution 78/103 on the report of the United Nations Commission on International Trade Law on the work of its fifty-sixth session, resolution 78/104 on the Model Provisions on Mediation for International Investment Disputes and Guidelines on Mediation for International Investment Disputes of the United Nations Commission on International Trade Law, resolution 78/105 on the Code of Conduct for Arbitrators in International Investment Dispute Resolution and Code of Conduct for Judges in International Investment Dispute Resolution with respective commentary of the United Nations Commission on International Trade Law, and resolution 78/106 on the Guide on Access to Credit for Micro-, Small and Medium-sized Enterprises of the United Nations Commission on International Trade Law.

370. The Commission took note of those General Assembly resolutions.

XIX. Other business

A. Evaluation of the role of the UNCITRAL secretariat in facilitating the work of the Commission

371. An online questionnaire on the level of satisfaction of UNCITRAL with the services provided by its secretariat had been sent to States. The Commission was informed that 66 responses had been received and that the level of satisfaction with the services provided by the secretariat remained high. On average, respondents gave a rating of 4.5 out of 5 for "the services and support provided to the Commission" and a rating of 4.3 out of 5 for "the availability of information on the UNCITRAL website".

372. The Commission expressed appreciation to its secretariat for its work.

[124] Ibid., *Seventy-seventh Session, Supplement No. 17* (A/77/17), para. 237; ibid., *Seventy-eighth Session, Supplement No. 17* (A/78/17), para. 217.

[125] Ibid.

[126] *Official Records of the General Assembly, Seventy-second Session, Supplement No. 17* (A/72/17), para. 480.

B. Other matters

373. During the meeting on 2 July 2024, the European Union signed the Mauritius Convention.[127]

XX. Date and place of future meetings

A. Fifty-eighth session of the Commission

374. The Commission approved the holding of its fifty-eighth session in Vienna, from 7 to 25 July 2025. Depending on the expected workload of the session, the secretariat was requested to optimize the duration of the session to the extent possible.

B. Sessions of working groups

375. The Commission considered conference service requirements in light of its work programme, reports of its working groups and a note by the Secretariat (A/CN.9/1180). It approved the following schedule of working group sessions in the second half of 2024 and in 2025, noting that the dates proposed below included the following significant holidays of the United Nations: 20 March 2025 – Nowruz (which would fall on the fourth day of the tentative dates for the forty-sixth session of Working Group VI); and 12 May 2025 – Day of Vesak (which would fall on the first day of the tentative dates for the sixty-sixth session of Working Group V). The Commission emphasized the need to ensure that tentative dates allocated to working groups should remain unchanged to the extent possible.

	Second half of 2024 (Vienna)	*First half of 2025 (New York)*	*Second half of 2025 (Vienna) (to be confirmed by the Commission at its fifty-eighth session, in 2025)*
Working Group I (to be decided)	–	–	Forty-second session 29 September–3 October 2025
Working Group II (Dispute Settlement)	Eightieth session 30 September–4 October 2024	Eighty-first session 3–7 February 2025	Eighty-second session 13–17 October 2025
Working Group III (Investor-State Dispute Settlement Reform)	Forty-ninth session 23–27 September 2024	Fiftieth session (Vienna) 20–24 January 2025 Fifty-first session Two days during the week of 17–21 February 2025 and 7–11 April 2025	Fifty-second session 22–26 September 2025
Working Group IV (Electronic Commerce)	Sixty-seventh session 18–22 November 2024	Sixty-eighth session 24–28 March 2025	Sixty-ninth session 20–24 October 2025
Working Group V (Insolvency Law)	Sixty-fifth session 16–20 December 2024	Sixty-sixth session 12–16 May 2025 (12 May 2025 falls on Day of Vesak)	Sixty-seventh session 10–14 November 2025
Working Group VI (Negotiable Cargo Documents)	Forty-fifth session 9–13 December 2024	Forty-sixth session 17–21 March 2025 (20 March 2025 falls on Nowruz)	Forty-seventh session 15–19 December 2025

[127] United Nations, *Treaty Series*, vol. 3208.

Annex I

UNCITRAL-UNIDROIT Model Law on Warehouse Receipts

Chapter I. Scope and general provisions

Article 1
Scope of application

1. This Law applies to warehouse receipts.

2. For the purposes of this Law, a warehouse receipt is an electronic record or paper document issued and signed by a warehouse operator by which the warehouse operator:

(a) Acknowledges holding the goods covered by it on behalf of the holder; and

(b) Promises to deliver the goods to the holder.

Article 2
Definitions

For the purposes of this Law:

1. "Depositor" means a person who deposits goods for storage with a warehouse operator.

2. "Electronic record" means information generated, communicated, received or stored by electronic means, including, where appropriate, all information logically associated with or otherwise linked together so as to become part of the record, whether generated contemporaneously or not.

3. "Holder" of a warehouse receipt means:

(a) In the case of a receipt that is issued to bearer or endorsed in blank, the person in control of the warehouse receipt:

(i) If the warehouse receipt is electronic, pursuant to a method used in accordance with article 6, paragraph 3; or

(ii) If the warehouse receipt is issued in paper form, by possession.

(b) In the case of a warehouse receipt that is issued to the order of a named person – that person, or the most recent endorsee, if in control of the receipt.

(i) If the warehouse receipt is electronic, pursuant to a method used in accordance with article 6, paragraph 3; or

(ii) If the warehouse receipt is issued in paper form, by possession;

(c) In the case of a non-negotiable warehouse receipt – the person to whom delivery of the goods is to be made in accordance with the terms of the receipt.

4. "Negotiable warehouse receipt" means a warehouse receipt that is issued:

(a) To the order of a named person; or

(b) To bearer.

5. "Non-negotiable warehouse receipt" means a warehouse receipt that is issued in favour of a named person only.

6. "Protected holder" means a person that satisfies the requirements of article 17, paragraph 1.

7. "Storage agreement" means an agreement between a warehouse operator and a depositor that sets out the terms on which the warehouse operator agrees to store goods.

8. "Warehouse operator" means a person who is in the business of storing goods for other persons.

Article 3
Non-derogation

The provisions of this Law may not be derogated from or varied by agreement.

Article 4
Interpretation

In the interpretation of this Law, regard is to be had to its international origin and the need to promote uniformity in its application.

Chapter II. Issuance and contents of a warehouse receipt; replacement and change of medium

Article 5
Obligation to issue a warehouse receipt

A warehouse operator shall issue a warehouse receipt in relation to goods after receiving them for storage if requested by the depositor in accordance with the terms of the storage agreement.

Article 6
Electronic warehouse receipt

1. For the issuance and use of an electronic warehouse receipt, a reliable method shall be used:

(a) To identify the electronic warehouse receipt;

(b) To render that electronic warehouse receipt capable of being subject to control from its issuance until it ceases to have any effect or validity; and

(c) To retain the integrity of that electronic warehouse receipt.

2. The criterion for assessing integrity shall be whether information contained in the electronic warehouse receipt, including any authorized change that arises from its issuance until it ceases to have any effect or validity, has remained complete and unaltered apart from any change that arises in the normal course of communication, storage and display.

3. An electronic warehouse receipt is subject to control if a reliable method is used:

(a) To establish exclusive control of that electronic warehouse receipt by a person;

(b) To identify that person as the person in control; and

(c) To transfer control over the electronic warehouse receipt.

Article 7
General reliability standard for electronic warehouse receipts

For the purposes of article 6, the method referred to shall be:

(a) As reliable as appropriate for the fulfilment of the function for which the method is being used, in light of all relevant circumstances, which may include:

(i) Any operational rules relevant to the assessment of reliability;

(ii) The assurance of data integrity;

(iii) The ability to prevent unauthorized access to and use of the system;

(iv) The security of hardware and software;

(v) The regularity and extent of audit by an independent body;

(vi) The existence of a declaration by a supervisory body, an accreditation body or a voluntary scheme regarding the reliability of the method;

(vii) Any applicable industry standard; or

(b) Proven in fact to have fulfilled the function by itself or together with further evidence.

Article 8
Representations by the depositor

By requesting the issuance of a warehouse receipt, the depositor represents to the warehouse operator and to the subsequent holders that:

(a) It has the authority to deposit the goods;

(b) It has the authority to request the issuance of a negotiable or non-negotiable warehouse receipt; and

(c) To the best of its knowledge, the goods are free of any rights or claims of third parties except as notified to the warehouse operator.

Article 9
Incorporation of the storage agreement in the warehouse receipt

1. A warehouse receipt may state that it includes some or all terms of the storage agreement. In that case, a copy of the storage agreement or of its relevant provisions shall be made available to potential transferees upon request by the current holder.

2. Notwithstanding paragraph 1, the warehouse operator may not invoke against a holder under article 15 any term of the storage agreement that is inconsistent with the express terms of the warehouse receipt.

Article 10
Information to be included in a warehouse receipt

1. A warehouse operator shall include the following information in a warehouse receipt:

(a) The words "warehouse receipt";

(b) If it is negotiable, the name of the person to whose order the receipt is issued or a statement that it is issued to bearer;

(c) If it is non-negotiable, the name of the person in whose favour it is issued;

(d) The name and address of the depositor;

(e) The name and address of the warehouse operator;

(f) A description of the goods and their quantity;

(g) The existence of any rights or claims of third parties to the goods notified by the depositor to the warehouse operator pursuant to article 8, subparagraph (c);

(h) The fixed period of the storage, if any;

(i) The place where the goods are stored;

(j) A unique identifier for the receipt;

(k) The date and place of issuance; and

(l) The date of the storage agreement.

2. A missing, incomplete or incorrect statement of the information required under paragraph 1 does not affect the validity of the warehouse receipt, but the warehouse operator is not relieved from any liability that it would have under other law to any person as a result of the statement being missing, incomplete or incorrect.

3. If a warehouse receipt does not include the information required under paragraph 1, subparagraphs (b) or (c), it is presumed to be a negotiable warehouse receipt that is issued to bearer.

Article 11
Additional information that may be included in a warehouse receipt

1. A warehouse operator may also include any other information in a warehouse receipt, such as:

(a) The name of the insurer, if any, who has insured the goods, the details of the insurance policy covering the goods and the insured value;

(b) The amount of the storage fees if they are a fixed amount or, if they are not a fixed amount, how the fees are calculated;

(c) The quality of the goods; or

(d) If the goods are fungible, whether the goods may be commingled.

2. An incorrect statement of the information referred to in paragraph 1 does not affect the validity of the warehouse receipt, but the warehouse operator is not relieved from any liability that it would have under other law to any person as a result of the statement being incorrect.

3. If a warehouse receipt covers fungible goods but does not state the quality of the goods, the goods are presumed to be of average quality.

Article 12
Goods in sealed packages and similar situations

1. If the warehouse operator has no practicable or commercially reasonable means of inspecting the goods or otherwise verifying the information provided by the depositor, the warehouse operator may describe the goods, including their type, quantity and quality:

(a) In accordance with information provided to it by the depositor, by a statement to that effect in the warehouse receipt; or

(b) In the case of goods in a sealed package, by a statement to the effect that the package is said to contain the described goods and that the warehouse operator otherwise has no knowledge of the contents or condition of the contents of the package.

2. A warehouse operator who describes goods in accordance with paragraph 1 shall not be liable for any loss suffered by any person as a result of the description being incomplete or incorrect, unless the warehouse operator knew or had reasonable grounds to believe that the description was incomplete or incorrect.

Article 13
Loss or destruction of a warehouse receipt

1. In the event of loss or destruction of a warehouse receipt, the holder at the time of loss or destruction may require the warehouse operator to issue a replacement warehouse receipt subject to reasonable requirements that the warehouse operator may establish as regards:

(a) Proof of the loss or destruction of the warehouse receipt;

(b) Proof of the holder's entitlement to the warehouse receipt;

(c) An indemnity in relation to the issuance of the replacement warehouse receipt, and security in support of that indemnity; and

(d) Reimbursement of costs incurred for the replacement of the warehouse receipt, unless the storage agreement provides otherwise.

2. In the case of an electronic warehouse receipt:

(a) "Loss or destruction" as referred to in paragraph 1 occurs when any of the conditions for the issuance and use of an electronic warehouse receipt set out in article 6, paragraph 1, or any of the conditions necessary for establishing the existence of control set out in article 6, paragraph 3, ceases to be met; and

(b) "Issue a replacement warehouse receipt" in paragraph 1 may include reinstatement of control of an electronic warehouse receipt over which control has been lost.

3. If a warehouse operator fails to issue a replacement warehouse receipt pursuant to paragraph 1, the holder at the time of loss or destruction may apply to the court for an order that the warehouse operator issue a replacement warehouse receipt, including by way of proceedings in the form of [*the enacting State specifies the appropriate expeditious proceedings*].

4. A replacement warehouse receipt issued under this article shall state that it is a replacement warehouse receipt and shall cancel and supersede the warehouse receipt believed to have been lost or destroyed.

5. Only the replacement warehouse receipt issued in accordance with paragraph 4 entitles the holder, or a person nominated by the holder, to claim delivery of the goods under article 26, but a person who, in good faith, acquires the warehouse receipt believed to have been lost or destroyed retains any right to claim damages from a previous holder that may be available under other law.

Article 14
Change of medium of a warehouse receipt

1. If the holder of a warehouse receipt so requests, a warehouse operator may change the medium of the warehouse receipt from paper to electronic or from electronic to paper.

2. At the time of the change of medium, the warehouse operator shall ensure that the warehouse receipt, in its previous medium, becomes inoperative and ceases to have any effect or validity.

3. The change of medium does not affect the rights and obligations of the parties.

Chapter III. Transfers and other dealings in negotiable warehouse receipts

Article 15
Transfer of a negotiable warehouse receipt

1. A paper negotiable warehouse receipt may be transferred:

(a) By endorsement and delivery, if it is issued or endorsed to the order of the person transferring it; or

(b) By delivery, if:

(i) It is issued to bearer; or

(ii) It is endorsed in blank or to bearer.

2. An electronic negotiable warehouse receipt may be transferred by transfer of control.

Article 16
Rights of a transferee generally

1. A person to whom a negotiable warehouse receipt has been transferred acquires:

(a) The benefit of the obligation of the warehouse operator to hold and deliver the goods in accordance with the terms of the receipt; and

(b) Such rights to the receipt and the goods as the transferor was able to convey.

2. Paragraph 1 does not limit the rights of a protected holder of a negotiable warehouse receipt pursuant to article 18.

Article 17
Protected holder of a negotiable warehouse receipt

1. A person is a protected holder of a negotiable warehouse receipt if:

(a) The receipt has been transferred to the person pursuant to article 15;

(b) The person acted in good faith and without knowledge of any right or claim to the receipt or the goods covered by it, or of any defence on the part of any person other than the warehouse operator; and

(c) The transfer was in the ordinary course of business or financing.

[2. A person does not have knowledge of a right or claim to a warehouse receipt or the goods covered by it for the purposes of paragraph 1, subparagraph (b), merely because information relating to that claim has been registered in [*the enacting State specifies the appropriate registry established pursuant to a secured transactions law*].][1]

3. If a negotiable warehouse receipt is issued by a warehouse operator to the order of a named person other than the depositor, the issuance of the receipt to that person by the warehouse operator has the same effect, for the purposes of determining whether that person is a protected holder, as if the receipt had been transferred to that person pursuant to article 15.

Article 18
Rights of a protected holder of a negotiable warehouse receipt[2]

Option 1

1. A protected holder of a negotiable warehouse receipt acquires ownership of the receipt and the goods covered by the receipt, and the benefit of the obligation of the warehouse operator to hold and deliver the goods in accordance with the terms of the receipt, free of any right, claim or defence of the warehouse operator or any other person, other than any right, claim or defence that arises under the terms of the receipt or under this Law.

Option 2

1. A protected holder of a negotiable warehouse receipt acquires:

(a) Ownership of the receipt and the benefit of the obligation of the warehouse operator to hold and deliver the goods in accordance with the terms of the receipt; and

---

[1] This provision appears within square brackets as not all enacting States may have a registry for the registration of notices with respect to security rights of the type envisaged in chapter IV of the UNCITRAL Model Law on Secured Transactions.

[2] The enacting State may wish to choose the option that better reflects the nature of the rights acquired by the protected holder of a document of title in respect of the goods covered by the document in its domestic legal system.

(b) Such rights to the goods as it would acquire by the transfer of physical possession of the goods under other law, free of any claim or defence of the warehouse operator or any other person, other than any claim or defence that arises under the terms of the receipt or under this Law.

2. Paragraph 1 applies even if:

(a) The transfer to the protected holder or any prior transfer constituted a breach of duty by the transferor;

(b) A previous holder of the receipt lost control or possession of the receipt as a result of fraud, duress, theft, misappropriation, misrepresentation, mistake, accident or similar circumstances; or

(c) The goods or the receipt had previously been sold, transferred or encumbered to a third person.

3. The rights of a protected holder of a negotiable warehouse receipt under paragraph 1 are not subject to [*the enacting State specifies any retention-of-title, security or equivalent right*] that any person may have in or in relation to the goods covered by the receipt.

4. The rights of a protected holder of a negotiable warehouse receipt under paragraph 1 are not subject to any right pursuant to a judgment against any other person. The warehouse operator is not obliged to deliver the goods to a person claiming pursuant to such a judgment, unless the warehouse receipt is surrendered to the warehouse operator.

Article 19
Third-party effectiveness of a security right

A security right in a negotiable warehouse receipt may be made effective against third parties by:

(a) [Registration in a registry established pursuant to [*the enacting State specifies its secured transactions law providing for such registry*];][3]

(b) In the case of an electronic negotiable warehouse receipt, the secured creditor taking control of the receipt; or

(c) In the case of a paper negotiable warehouse receipt, the secured creditor taking possession of the receipt.

Article 20
Representations by a transferor of a negotiable warehouse receipt

A transferor of a negotiable warehouse receipt represents to the transferee that:

(a) The receipt is authentic; and

(b) The transferor does not know of any fact that would impair the validity of the receipt, the value of the goods covered by the receipt, or the effectiveness of the transfer of the receipt and rights to the goods it covers, except as notified to the transferee.

Article 21
Limited representation by intermediaries

An intermediary that is known to be entrusted with a warehouse receipt on behalf of another person may exercise all rights arising out of the receipt but

[3] This provision appears within square brackets as not all enacting States may have a registry for the registration of notices with respect to security rights of the type envisaged in chapter IV of the UNCITRAL Model Law on Secured Transactions.

represents by the transfer of a negotiable warehouse receipt only that it is authorized to do so and does not make the representations referred to in article 20.

Article 22
Transferor not responsible for the warehouse operators' performance

A person who transfers a negotiable warehouse receipt does not guarantee, by virtue of the transfer, the performance by the warehouse operator of any obligations evidenced by the receipt.

Chapter IV. Rights and obligations of the warehouse operator

Article 23
Duty of care

1. The warehouse operator shall store and preserve the goods in accordance with the level of care expected of a diligent and competent warehouse operator storing goods of that type.

2. The warehouse receipt may contain limitations on and conditions to the obligations of the warehouse operator under this chapter, but any clause purporting to lower the duty of care in paragraph 1 or to exclude or limit the warehouse operator's liability for its fraud, wilful misconduct, gross negligence or misappropriation of the goods shall be null and void. The invalidity of such a clause shall not otherwise affect the validity of the warehouse receipt.

Article 24
Duty to keep goods separate

1. Subject to paragraph 2, the warehouse operator shall keep the goods covered by each receipt separate so as to permit identification of the goods at any time.

2. The warehouse operator may commingle fungible goods into a mass of goods of the same type and quality, to the extent permitted by the warehouse receipt.

Article 25
Lien of the warehouse operator

1. The warehouse operator has a lien on the goods in its possession and in any proceeds for:

(a) Charges for storage of the goods;

(b) Unexpected reasonable expenses necessary for the preservation of the goods;

(c) Reasonable expenses incurred in the sale of the goods in accordance with paragraph 4; and

(d) Similar charges or expenses owed by the holder in relation to other goods held by the warehouse operator, if so stated in the warehouse receipt.

2. Subject to paragraph 3, the warehouse operator's lien is effective against third parties.

3. As against a protected holder, the lien is limited to:

(a) Charges and expenses expressly stated in the warehouse receipt; or

(b) If no charges or expenses are so stated, a reasonable charge for storage after the date of issuance of the receipt.

4. The warehouse operator may enforce its lien pursuant to [*relevant other law as specified by the enacting State*].

Article 26
Obligation of the warehouse operator to deliver

1. Except as provided in article 29, the warehouse operator shall deliver the goods to the holder, or a person nominated by the holder, if the holder:

(a) Provides the warehouse operator with an instruction to deliver the goods;

(b) Surrenders the warehouse receipt to the warehouse operator; and

(c) Pays any outstanding amounts owed to the warehouse operator in respect of any of the charges or expenses referred to in article 25, paragraph 1, or, in the case of a protected holder, those referred to in article 25, paragraph 3.

2. Upon delivery of the goods, the warehouse operator shall cancel the warehouse receipt.

Article 27
Partial delivery

1. Except as provided in article 29, the warehouse operator shall deliver part of the goods to the holder, or a person nominated by the holder, if the holder:

(a) Provides the warehouse operator with an instruction as to the delivery of the goods;

(b) Surrenders the warehouse receipt to the warehouse operator; and

(c) Pays a corresponding proportion of any outstanding amounts owed to the warehouse operator in respect of any of the charges or expenses referred to in article 25, paragraph 1, or, in the case of a protected holder, those referred to in article 25, paragraph 3.

2. Upon partial delivery of the goods, the warehouse operator shall note the partial delivery on the warehouse receipt and return the receipt to the holder.

Article 28
Split warehouse receipts

1. If requested by the holder of a warehouse receipt, a warehouse operator shall split the warehouse receipt into two or more warehouse receipts that cover the totality of the goods that were covered by the original warehouse receipt, upon surrender of the original warehouse receipt and payment of any additional cost reasonably incurred by the warehouse operator as a consequence of the split and reissuance of the warehouse receipt, unless the storage agreement provides otherwise.

2. Upon issuance of the split warehouse receipts, the warehouse operator shall cancel the original warehouse receipt.

Article 29
Exoneration from delivery obligation

The warehouse operator is relieved of its obligation to deliver the goods if and to the extent it establishes any of the following:

(a) Destruction or loss of the goods for which the warehouse operator is not liable;

(b) That it has sold or otherwise disposed of the goods in enforcement of its lien pursuant to article 25, paragraph 4, or to article 30; or

(c) That it is prevented from doing so by court order or otherwise by circumstances beyond its control.

Article 30
Termination of storage by the warehouse operator

1. The warehouse operator, by giving notice to all persons known to the warehouse operator to claim an interest in the goods, may:

(a) Demand payment of the amounts secured by its lien and removal of the goods by the end of the storage period specified in the warehouse receipt or, if the storage period has expired or no storage period is specified in the warehouse receipt, within a reasonable period [of not less than ... days [*the enacting State specifies a certain period*]] after the warehouse operator gives notice, as specified in the notice; and

(b) Reserve the right, if the amounts are not paid and the goods not removed by the date or within the period specified in the notice, to then sell the goods in any commercially reasonable manner.

2. If the warehouse operator determines in good faith that, within the time provided in paragraph 1, subparagraph (a), the goods will deteriorate or decline in value to less than the amount secured by its lien, the warehouse operator may specify in the notice given under paragraph 1, subparagraph (a), any reasonably shorter time for removal of the goods and, if the goods are not removed, may sell them in accordance with paragraph 1, subparagraph (b).

3. If the warehouse operator does not know of any person claiming an interest in the goods, the notice required under this article may be given by public advertisement pursuant to [*relevant other law as specified by the enacting State*].

4. If, as a result of a quality or condition of the goods about which the warehouse operator neither knew nor ought to have known at the time of deposit, the goods are a hazard, the warehouse operator may dispose of the goods in any lawful manner.

[Chapter V. Pledge bonds][4]

Article 31
Scope of provisions on pledge bonds

This chapter governs the effects of the pledge bond once transferred separately from the warehouse receipt.

Article 32
Issuance and form of a pledge bond

1. The warehouse operator shall issue a pledge bond as a paper document signed by the warehouse operator that is associated with, but detachable from, the warehouse receipt, or as an electronic record capable of being controlled separately from the electronic warehouse receipt, which, once detached or subject to separate control:

(a) Represents the holder's right to payment of the amount stated in the pledge bond; and

(b) Grants the holder of the pledge bond a security right in the goods covered by the warehouse receipt.

2. The pledge bond shall identify itself as a pledge bond rather than as a warehouse receipt, but shall otherwise contain the same information as the warehouse receipt to which it relates.

[4] This chapter is offered to States that wish to introduce or modernize a "dual" system of warehouse receipts consisting of two documents capable of being transferred separately. An enacting State that wishes to maintain or introduce a dual warehouse receipt system could enact this chapter either in its current form or integrated with the contents of the main body of the Model Law. The chapter appears within square brackets to enable States that wish to maintain or introduce a single warehouse receipt system not to incorporate chapter V in their legislation.

3. "Holder" of a pledge bond means:

(a) In the case of a pledge bond that is issued to bearer or endorsed in blank, the person in control of the pledge bond:

(i) If the pledge bond is electronic, pursuant to a method used in accordance with article 6, paragraph 3; or

(ii) If the pledge bond is issued in paper form, by possession;

(b) In the case of a pledge bond that is issued to the order of a named person – that person, or the most recent endorsee, if in control of the pledge bond:

(i) If the pledge bond is electronic, pursuant to a method used in accordance with article 6, paragraph 3; or

(ii) If the pledge bond is issued in paper form, by possession.

4. Except for article 10, paragraph 1, subparagraph (a), articles 5 to 14 apply in relation to pledge bonds in the same way as they apply to warehouse receipts.

Article 33
Effect of a pledge bond

1. The rights of the holder of the warehouse receipt to goods are subject to the rights of the holder of the pledge bond.

2. The holder of the warehouse receipt may pay the amounts secured by the pledge bond to its holder whether or not the amount is yet due, in which case the holder of the pledge bond shall surrender the pledge bond to the holder of the warehouse receipt.

3. If there has been default in payment of the amount secured by a pledge bond, the holder of the pledge bond may enforce its security right over the goods pursuant to [*relevant other law as specified by the enacting State*].

Article 34
Transfers and other dealings

1. A pledge bond may be transferred together with the warehouse receipt, or separately. When transferred separately from the warehouse receipt, the pledge bond transfers the rights referred to in article 32, paragraph 1, subparagraphs (a) and (b).

2. The first holder of a pledge bond to transfer it separately from the warehouse receipt shall ensure that:

(a) The amount secured by the pledge bond and the due date for payment are inserted in the pledge bond; and

(b) Such information is transcribed into the warehouse receipt and a copy of the completed warehouse receipt is provided to the warehouse operator.

3. Articles 15 to 18 and 20 to 22 apply to pledge bonds in the same way as they apply to warehouse receipts.

Article 35
Rights and obligations of the warehouse operator

1. If the pledge bond has been transferred separately from the warehouse receipt, the warehouse operator shall only split the warehouse receipt in accordance with article 28 if requested by both the holder of the warehouse receipt and the holder of the pledge bond.

2. Prior to the due date for payment of the amount secured by the pledge bond, the warehouse operator shall only deliver all or part of the goods upon presentation of both the warehouse receipt and the pledge bond.

3. After the due date for payment of the amount secured by the pledge bond, the warehouse operator shall deliver the goods upon presentation of the pledge bond whether or not the warehouse receipt is also surrendered.

Chapter VI. Application of this Law

Article 36
Entry into force

1. This Law enters into force [*on the date or according to a mechanism to be specified by the enacting State*].

2. This Law applies to warehouse receipts [and pledge bonds] that are issued after this Law enters into force.

Article 37
Repeal and amendment of other laws

1. [*The laws as specified by the enacting State*] are repealed.

2. [*The laws as specified by the enacting State*] are amended as follows [*the text of the relevant amendments to be specified by the enacting State*].

Annex II

UNCITRAL Model Clauses on Specialized Express Dispute Resolution

Model Clause on Highly Expedited Arbitration

Any dispute, controversy or claim arising out of or relating to this contract, or the breach, termination or invalidity thereof, shall be settled by arbitration in accordance with the UNCITRAL Expedited Arbitration Rules ("Expedited Rules"), with the following modifications:

(a) The period of time for the parties to reach an agreement on the appointment of a sole arbitrator in article 8 (2) of the Expedited Rules shall be [7] days after a proposal has been received by all other parties;

(b) The appointing authority shall be [name of institution or person];

(c) The period of time within which the arbitral tribunal shall consult the parties on the manner in which it will conduct the arbitration pursuant to article 9 of the Expedited Rules shall be [7] days;

(d) The period of time within which the award shall be made pursuant to article 16 (1) of the Expedited Rules shall be [45] days;

(e)

Option I: The extended period of time in article 16 (2) of the Expedited Rules shall not exceed a total of [90] days;

OR

Option II: The extended period of time in article 16 (2) of the Expedited Rules shall not exceed a total of [90] days. The period of time within which the award shall be made may not be further extended, and article 16 (3) and (4) of the Expedited Rules shall not apply;

(f) The power of the arbitral tribunal pursuant to article 2 (2) of the Expedited Rules to determine that the Expedited Rules shall no longer apply to the arbitration also extends to the power to determine that the modifications to the Expedited Rules contained herein shall no longer apply.

Model Clause on Adjudication

Note: Parties entering into a contractual relationship may wish to adopt the following procedure whereby disputes, as and when they arise, can be resolved in an expedited and binding manner by an adjudicator, subject to any party's right to have the same dispute finally resolved in an arbitration.

Arbitration

1. Any dispute, controversy or claim arising out of or relating to this contract, or breach, termination or invalidity thereof ("Dispute"), shall be settled by arbitration in accordance with the UNCITRAL Arbitration Rules with the following additions:

(a) The appointing authority shall be... [name of institution or person];

(b) The number of arbitrators shall be... [one or three];

(c) The place of the arbitration shall be... [town and country];

(d) The language to be used in the arbitral proceedings shall be....

Adjudication

Option I		*Option II*
2. Any Dispute may be determined by adjudication in accordance with the following subparagraphs.	OR	2. Any Dispute relating to [certain possible disputes under the contract*] may be determined by adjudication in accordance with the following subparagraphs. Any disagreement as to whether a dispute referred to the adjudicator falls within the limited scope specified by the parties in the prior sentence shall be resolved by the adjudicator.

(a) A party initiating adjudication shall communicate a request for adjudication containing a description of the dispute, including its basis and an indication of the determination being requested to all other parties and, once there is an agreement on his or her appointment, to the adjudicator;

(b) If the parties have not reached an agreement on an impartial and independent adjudicator [7] days after a proposal made by a party has been received by all other parties, the adjudicator shall, at the request of any party, be appointed promptly by the appointing authority;

(c) The appointing authority for the adjudicator shall be... [name of institution or person];

(d) The adjudicator shall consult with the parties on matters related to the dispute and the procedure promptly and within 3 days of his or her acceptance of appointment for the dispute. The adjudicator may hold additional consultations with the parties on matters related to the dispute or request additional information from the parties as he or she deems necessary;

(e) Within [14] days of the acceptance of appointment for the dispute by the adjudicator, the other party or parties shall communicate a response to the request;

(f) Subject to subparagraph (h), the adjudicator may conduct the proceedings as he or she considers appropriate, including abridging or extending any period of time, provided that the parties are treated with equality and that each party is given a reasonable opportunity to present its case;

(g) The adjudicator may determine that the dispute is, in whole or in part, not suitable for adjudication;

(h) The adjudicator shall make the determination within [30] days of the acceptance of appointment for the dispute by the adjudicator stating the reasons. In exceptional circumstances and after having consulted the parties, the adjudicator may extend the period of time for making the determination, which shall not exceed a total of [60] days;

(i) The determination of the adjudicator shall be binding on the parties and the parties shall comply with the determination without delay.

Compliance Arbitration

3. Any dispute as to the compliance by any of the parties with the determination of the adjudicator under paragraph 2 (i) may be referred to arbitration by either party,

* For example, claims solely for monetary relief.

in accordance with the UNCITRAL Expedited Arbitration Rules ("Expedited Rules"), with the following modifications:

(a) The period of time for the parties to reach an agreement on the appointment of a sole arbitrator in article 8 (2) of the Expedited Rules shall be [7] days after a proposal has been received by all other parties;

(b) The period of time within which the arbitral tribunal shall consult the parties on the manner in which it will conduct the arbitration pursuant to article 9 of the Expedited Rules shall be [7] days;

(c) The period of time within which the award shall be made pursuant to article 16 (1) of the Expedited Rules shall be [30] days;

(d) The extended period of time referred to in article 16 (2) of the Expedited Rules shall not exceed a total of [60] days. The period of time within which the award shall be made may not be further extended, and article 16 (3) and (4) of the Expedited Rules shall not apply;

(e) The arbitral tribunal shall limit the proceedings to deciding whether a party has breached its undertaking in paragraph 2 (i) and, if so, to ordering compliance with the determination of the adjudicator, unless it finds that the adjudicator failed to comply with paragraph 2 (f). The arbitral tribunal shall not review the merits of the determination of the adjudicator.

Arbitration under paragraph 1 in relation to adjudication

4. In any arbitration initiated by the parties under paragraph 1:

(a) A party may submit disputes considered in the adjudication under paragraph 2 without being limited by any of its claims, arguments, evidence or other submissions in the adjudication; and

(b) The arbitral tribunal shall not be bound by any determination made by the adjudicator.

5. The initiation of adjudication and arbitration under paragraphs 2 and 3 shall not preclude the initiation or continuation of arbitration under paragraph 1 with respect to any dispute. Similarly, the initiation of arbitration under paragraph 1 shall not preclude the initiation or continuation of adjudication and arbitration under paragraphs 2 and 3 of any dispute.

Optional addition to paragraph 5: Once adjudication has been initiated and is continuing, arbitration under paragraph 1 on issues before the adjudicator may be commenced only once the adjudicator has made his or her determination. If adjudication is initiated while arbitral proceedings are continuing, the arbitral proceedings on issues before the adjudicator, at the request of a party, shall be suspended until the adjudicator has made his or her determination.

Model Clause on Technical Advisors

1. The arbitral tribunal may appoint one or more independent technical advisors to accompany it in the proceedings and, as the need arises, to assist it in the technical understanding of the dispute.

2. In the process of selecting and appointing a technical advisor, the arbitral tribunal shall consult the parties on:

(a) The specific area of technical expertise necessary;

(b) The terms of reference, including the type of assistance to be provided by the technical advisor and the means and manner in which the technical advisor performs his or her role; and

(c) Any additional matters that the arbitral tribunal deems pertinent.

3. Article 29 (2) of the UNCITRAL Arbitration Rules shall apply to technical advisors.

4. The arbitral tribunal shall ensure that the parties are given a reasonable opportunity to comment on the explanations provided by the technical advisor.

Model Clause on Confidentiality**

1. Each party shall maintain the confidentiality of all aspects of the proceedings, including the existence of the proceedings, all non-public information disclosed by another party in the proceedings, all non-public decisions or awards, [and any decisions or awards that have been proven to have become public unlawfully] with the following exceptions: to the extent that such disclosure is required by legal duty, to protect or pursue a legal right or interest, or in relation to enforcing or challenging awards in legal proceedings before a court or other competent authority, or for the purposes of having, or seeking, legal, accounting or other professional services.

2. The arbitral tribunal and the parties shall seek the same undertaking of confidentiality in writing from all those that they involve in the proceedings.

3. The arbitral tribunal may, upon the request of a party, make orders concerning the confidentiality of the arbitral proceedings and take measures for protecting confidential information.

** In some jurisdictions, a valid confidentiality agreement can only be concluded once a dispute has arisen. In such cases, parties may add the following first paragraph to the Model Clause: "Upon commencement of a dispute, parties may consider agreeing on the following:" (and then include the Model Clause as it currently stands).

Annex III

Statute of the Advisory Centre on International Investment Dispute Resolution (adopted in principle)

Article 1
Establishment

The Advisory Centre on International Investment Dispute Resolution (hereinafter, the "Advisory Centre") is hereby established.

Article 2
Objectives

1. The Advisory Centre aims to provide training, support and assistance with regard to international investment dispute resolution.

2. The Advisory Centre aims to enhance the capacity of States and regional economic integration organizations to prevent and handle international investment disputes, in particular least developed countries and developing countries.

Article 3
General principles

1. The Advisory Centre shall operate in a manner that is effective, affordable, accessible and financially sustainable.

2. The Advisory Centre shall be independent and free from undue external influence, including from its donors.

3. The Advisory Centre shall, as appropriate, cooperate with international and regional organizations and coordinate its activities to ensure the efficient use of its resources.

Article 4
Membership

1. A State or a regional economic integration organization may become a Member of the Advisory Centre in accordance with article 12.

2. Each Member is entitled to the services of the Advisory Centre and has obligations, as set out in this Protocol and the regulations adopted by the Governing Committee.

3. For the purposes of this Protocol, each Member shall be categorized into [annex I, annex II or annex III]. This categorization is without prejudice to classifications in other instruments or other organizations.

4. For the purposes of this Protocol, a "non-Member" refers to a State or a regional economic integration organization that is not a Party to this Protocol.

Article 5
Structure

1. The Advisory Centre shall consist of a Governing Committee, an Executive Committee and a Secretariat headed by an Executive Director.

Governing Committee

2. The Governing Committee shall be composed of representatives of the Members of the Advisory Centre. Each Member shall appoint one representative to the Governing Committee.

3. The Governing Committee shall:

(a) Adopt and publish its rules of procedure and those of the Executive Committee;

(b) Adopt and publish regulations on the operation of the Advisory Centre;

(c) Appoint the members of the Executive Committee taking into consideration geographical diversity and gender balance;

(d) Assign any other functions to the Executive Committee;

(e) Adopt and publish the staff regulations on the conditions of services and rights and obligations of the Executive Director and staff members of the Secretariat;

(f) Appoint the Executive Director for a term of four (4) years; the Executive Director shall be eligible for reappointment;

(g) Evaluate and monitor the performance of the Advisory Centre and adopt and publish the annual report prepared by the Executive Director;

(h) Adopt and publish the annual budget of the Advisory Centre prepared by the Executive Director and reviewed by the Executive Committee;

(i) Periodically assess and, if needed, adjust the scope and type of services of the Advisory Centre, including by deciding to phase in some of the services at a later stage of its operation; and

(j) Perform other functions in accordance with this Protocol.

4. The Governing Committee shall meet at least once a year.

Executive Committee

5. The Executive Committee shall consist of [six] members. The Executive Director shall also serve ex officio on the Executive Committee. Each group of Members listed in [annexes I, II and III] shall nominate [two] members of the Executive Committee for appointment by the Governing Committee. The members of the Executive Committee shall serve in their personal capacity and shall be selected on the basis of their professional qualifications, including in particular in international investment dispute resolution.

6. The Executive Committee shall be accountable to the Governing Committee. The Executive Committee shall meet as often as necessary and shall:

(a) Propose for adoption by the Governing Committee rules on the procedure of the Executive Committee;

(b) Take decisions necessary to ensure the efficient and effective operation of the Advisory Centre in accordance with this Protocol and the regulations adopted by the Governing Committee;

(c) Review the annual budget of the Advisory Centre prepared by the Executive Director and submit it for adoption by the Governing Committee;

(d) Provide advice to the Executive Director, including on the administration of the budget of the Advisory Centre;

(e) Appoint the external auditor;

(f) Supervise the administration of the Secretariat; and

(g) Perform other functions in accordance with this Protocol and as assigned by the Governing Committee.

Decision-making

7. The Governing Committee and the Executive Committee shall endeavour to make all decisions by consensus.

8. If a decision cannot be made by consensus in the Governing Committee, the subject matter may be submitted to a vote, which requires the presence of a majority of the Members. Each Member shall have one vote. Decisions shall require a four-fifths majority of the Members present and voting. If the majority of the Members are not present, the same subject matter may be submitted for a second vote at the next meeting of the Governing Committee, the decision of which may be made by a four-fifths majority of the Members present and voting.

9. If a decision cannot be made by consensus in the Executive Committee, the subject matter may be submitted to a vote, which requires the presence of a majority of the members of the Executive Committee. Each member shall have one vote and the Executive Director, serving ex officio, shall not have a vote. Decisions shall require a four-fifths majority of the members present and voting. If the majority of the members are not present, the same subject matter may be submitted for a second vote at the next meeting of the Executive Committee, the decision of which may be made by a four-fifths majority of the members present and voting.

Executive Director and the Secretariat

10. The Executive Director shall:

(a) Manage the day-to-day operation of the Advisory Centre;

(b) Employ and manage the staff members of the Secretariat in accordance with the staff regulations adopted by the Governing Committee;

(c) Prepare the annual report on the operation of the Advisory Centre for adoption by the Governing Committee;

(d) Prepare the annual budget of the Advisory Centre for review by the Executive Committee; and

(e) Represent the Advisory Centre externally.

11. The Executive Director shall be accountable to the Governing Committee.

12. The Executive Director shall not hold any other employment or engage in any other occupation without the approval of the Executive Committee.

Article 6
Technical assistance and capacity-building

1. The Advisory Centre shall provide technical assistance to its Members and engage in capacity-building activities with regard to international investment dispute resolution, including by:

(a) Advising on issues pertaining to dispute prevention;

(b) Providing tailored training with regard to possible means of preventing and resolving disputes;

(c) Holding seminars and conferences;

(d) Functioning as a forum for the exchange of information and sharing of best practices;

(e) Functioning as a repository of information and related resources; and

(f) Performing any other functions as assigned by the Governing Committee.

2. The Advisory Centre may engage other persons or entities in providing the services in paragraph 1.

3. In accordance with the regulations adopted by the Governing Committee, the Executive Director may allow:

(a) Non-Members to participate in the activities organized by the Advisory Centre pursuant to paragraph 1; and

(b) Other persons or entities to participate in the activities pursuant to paragraph 1, subparagraphs (c) to (e). When the Governing Committee assigns any other functions in accordance with paragraph 1, subparagraph (f), it shall also determine the extent to which the Executive Director may allow other persons or entities to participate in those activities.

4. The regulations adopted by the Governing Committee shall require the Executive Director to set appropriate fees for the participation of non-Members, other persons or entities, and include criteria for allowing participation, such as whether it contributes to the objectives of the Advisory Centre, whether it creates any conflict of interest and the resource implications for the Advisory Centre.

Article 7
Legal advice and support with regard to international investment dispute proceedings

1. Upon request by a Member, the Advisory Centre shall provide legal support and advice with regard to an international investment dispute proceeding prior to and after its initiation, including by:

(a) Providing a preliminary assessment of the case, including the appropriate means to resolve the dispute;

(b) Assisting in the selection of mediators, arbitrators or other types of adjudicators (including any challenge), as well as experts, taking into account geographical diversity and gender balance;

(c) Supporting the preparation of statements, pleadings and evidence, as well as other aspects of the proceeding;

(d) Representing the Member in the proceeding, including in a hearing, at the instruction of and in conjunction with that Member;

(e) Facilitating the appointment of external legal representatives; and

(f) Performing any other functions as assigned by the Governing Committee.

2. The provision of services in paragraph 1 is subject to the resources available to the Advisory Centre.

3. In providing the services in paragraph 1, the Advisory Centre shall, in principle, give priority to Members listed in [annex I], followed by Members listed in [annex II], in accordance with the regulations adopted by the Governing Committee. In the event that requests are received from Members listed in the same annex, priority shall generally be given to the Member that requested the services first.

4. The Executive Director may allow a non-Member to request the services in paragraph 1 in accordance with the regulations adopted by the Governing Committee. Whether the requesting non-Member may benefit from the services and the extent of the services to be provided by the Advisory Centre shall be determined by the Governing Committee. In making the determination, the Governing Committee shall consider whether allowing a non-Member to benefit from the services contributes to the objectives of the Advisory Centre, whether the non-Member is in the process of becoming a Member, whether it creates any conflict of interest and the resource implications for the Advisory Centre.

Article 8
Financing

1. The operation of the Advisory Centre shall be funded by the contributions of Members, the fees for services provided by the Advisory Centre and voluntary contributions.

2. Each Member shall make financial contributions in accordance with [annex IV]. If a Member is in default of its contributions, the Governing Committee may decide to limit or modify its rights or obligations in accordance with the criteria established in the regulations adopted by the Governing Committee.

3. The Advisory Centre shall charge fees for its services in accordance with the regulations adopted by the Governing Committee:

(a) Services in article 6, paragraph 1, shall be provided at no cost to Members. The fees to be charged to non-Members, other persons and entities shall be determined by the Executive Director in accordance with the regulations adopted by the Governing Committee;

(b) The fees to be charged by the Advisory Centre for services in article 7, paragraph 1, shall not exceed the amount necessary to recover its costs. The fees to be charged to Members listed in [annex I] shall be lower than those charged to Members listed in [annex II], which shall be lower than those charged to Members listed in [annex III]. The fees to be charged to non-Members shall be equal to or higher than those charged to Members listed in [annex III], unless determined otherwise by the Governing Committee.

4. The Advisory Centre may receive voluntary contributions, whether monetary or in kind, from Members, non-Members, international and regional organizations and other persons or entities in accordance with the regulations adopted by the Governing Committee, provided that the receipt of such contributions is consistent with the objectives of the Advisory Centre, is reported in the annual report and does not create any conflict of interest or otherwise impede the independent operation of the Advisory Centre.

5. The Advisory Centre may set up trust funds for the purposes of receiving and managing the financial contributions and the fees referred to in paragraphs 1 to 4.

6. The budget and expenditure of the Advisory Centre shall be subject to internal and external audit.

Article 9
Legal status and liability

1. The Advisory Centre shall have full international legal personality. The legal capacity of the Advisory Centre shall include the capacity to contract, to acquire and dispose of immovable and movable property and to institute legal proceedings.

2. The Advisory Centre shall be headquartered in [*to be determined*]. The Advisory Centre shall conclude a host country agreement with [*host State/Government to be determined*]. The Governing Committee may decide to relocate the headquarters, either temporarily or permanently, in the event that exceptional circumstances so significantly impact the operational effectiveness of the headquarters that the existing location is no longer suitable.

3. The Governing Committee may decide to establish regional offices of the Advisory Centre.

4. To fulfil its objectives, the Advisory Centre shall enjoy in the territories of each Member the privileges and immunities as set out in this Protocol.

5. The archives of the Advisory Centre shall be inviolable, wherever they may be.

6. The Advisory Centre, its property and assets shall enjoy, at a minimum, such immunity as necessary for the fulfilment of its objectives and for the exercise of its functions, except when the Advisory Centre waives this immunity.

7. The Advisory Centre, its property, assets and income, and its operations and transactions authorized by this Protocol shall be exempt from direct taxation and all customs duties. The Advisory Centre shall also be exempt from liability for the collection or payment of any taxes or customs duties.

8. The Executive Director and staff members of the Secretariat shall enjoy immunity from legal process with respect to acts performed by them in the exercise of their functions, except when the Advisory Centre waives this immunity.

9. No tax shall be levied on or in respect of salaries, expense allowances or other emoluments paid by the Advisory Centre to the Executive Director and the staff members of the Secretariat.

Article 10
Reservations

No reservations are permitted under this Protocol.

Article 11
Depositary

The [*to be determined*] is hereby designated as the depositary of the Protocol.

Article 12
Signature, ratification, acceptance, approval, accession

1. This Protocol is open for signature by a State or a regional economic integration organization [*place and time to be determined*].

2. This Protocol is subject to ratification, acceptance or approval by the signatories.

3. This Protocol is open for accession by a State or a regional economic integration organization that is not a signatory from the date it is open for signature.

4. Instruments of ratification, acceptance, approval or accession are to be deposited with the depositary.

Article 13
Entry into force

1. This Protocol shall enter into force six months following the date upon which the following conditions are met:

(a) [*Number to be determined, including the possibility of requiring a certain number from each group of Members*] instruments of ratification, acceptance, approval or accession have been deposited; and

(b) The total amount of contributions that States or regional economic integration organizations that are Parties to the Protocol are obliged to make in accordance with [annex IV] exceeds [*an amount to be determined*].

2. When a State or a regional economic integration organization ratifies, accepts, approves or accedes to this Protocol after its entry into force in accordance with paragraph 1, this Protocol enters into force in respect of that State or regional economic integration organization thirty (30) days after the date of deposit of its instrument of ratification, acceptance, approval or accession.

Article 14
Annexes

The Annexes to this Protocol constitute an integral part of this Protocol.

Article 15
Amendments to the Protocol and annexes

Amendments to an article of the Protocol

1. Any Member may submit a proposal to amend an article of this Protocol to the Governing Committee. The proposal shall be promptly communicated to all Members. The Governing Committee may adopt the amendment in accordance with article 5, paragraphs 7 and 8.

2. The Executive Director shall communicate the amendment adopted pursuant to paragraph 1 to the depositary. The depositary shall submit the adopted amendment to all Members for ratification, acceptance or approval. The adopted amendment shall enter into force thirty (30) days after the date of deposit of the instrument of ratification, acceptance or approval by all Members.

Amendments to the Annexes

3. Any Member, the Executive Committee or the Executive Director may submit a proposal to amend [annexes I, II, III or IV] to the Governing Committee. The proposal shall be promptly communicated to all Members.

4. The Governing Committee shall adopt amendments to [annexes I, II and III] in accordance with article 5, paragraphs 7 and 8, only:

(a) To reflect in [annexes I and II] any changes to the list of least developed countries adopted by the United Nations General Assembly;

(b) To include in [annex II or III] a State listed in [annex I] that requests to be thus included;

(c) To include in [annex III] a State listed in [annex II] that requests to be thus included; or

(d) [*To refer to the possible use of objective criteria to be developed for classifying Members into [annexes II and III] in making adjustments thereto*].

5. The Governing Committee shall endeavour to adopt amendments to [annex IV] by consensus. If a decision cannot be made by consensus, the amendment shall be submitted for a vote to each group of Members listed in [annexes I, II and III]. The amendment shall be adopted when each group of Members adopts the amendment in accordance with article 5, paragraphs 7 and 8.

6. The Executive Director shall communicate the amendment adopted pursuant to paragraphs 4 and 5 to the depositary. The adopted amendment shall enter into force thirty (30) days after the notification is received by the depositary.

Party to the Protocol as amended

7. A State or a regional economic integration organization that becomes a Party to this Protocol after the entry into force of an amendment shall be considered a Party to the Protocol as amended.

Article 16
Withdrawal and termination

1. Any Member may at any time withdraw from this Protocol by means of a formal notification addressed to the depositary. The depositary shall inform the Executive Director, who shall promptly communicate the withdrawal to all Members. The withdrawal shall take effect thirty (30) days after the notification is received by the depositary. The obligations to make any remaining contribution at the time of withdrawal and to pay fees for the services provided by the Advisory Centre shall not

be affected by the withdrawal. The withdrawing Member shall not be entitled to any reimbursement of its contributions.

2. If a Member submits the notification of withdrawal within three (3) months of the date of receipt by the depositary of the notification of an amendment to any of the annexes, the amendment shall not apply to that Member.

3. The Governing Committee may terminate this Protocol. Upon termination, the assets of the Advisory Centre shall be distributed among the Members at that time in proportion to the total of each Member's contributions, including its voluntary contributions, to the financing of the Advisory Centre's operation.

Annexes

Annex I

[*This Annex would reflect the list of least developed countries adopted by the United Nations General Assembly when the statute is finalized.*]

Annexes [II and III]

[*Annexes [II and III] would list the States Members of the United Nations not listed in annex I. Those States would be categorized in accordance with the objective criteria to be developed for that purpose. The lists would also include regional economic integration organizations.*]

Annex [IV] – Scale of minimum contributions

	Annual contribution	Multi-year contribution	One-time contribution
Members listed in [annex I]			
Members listed in [annex II]			
Members listed in [annex III]			

Annex IV

UNCITRAL Model Law on Automated Contracting

Article 1
Definitions

1. For the purposes of this Law:

(a) "Automated system" means a computer system that is capable of carrying out actions without the necessary review or intervention of a natural person;

(b) "Data message" means information generated, sent, received or stored by electronic, magnetic, optical or similar means.

2. An automated system may be programmed to operate in a deterministic or non-deterministic manner.

Article 2
Scope of application

1. This Law applies to the use of automated systems to form or to perform contracts, including by:

(a) Generating or otherwise processing data messages that constitute an action in connection with the formation of contracts, such as an offer or acceptance of an offer;

(b) Generating or otherwise processing data messages that constitute an action in connection with the performance of a contract, such as its modification or termination.

2. Nothing in this Law affects the application of any rule of law that may govern the design, commissioning, operation or use of automated systems.

Article 3
Interpretation

1. In the interpretation of this Law, regard is to be had to its international origin and to the need to promote uniformity in its application and the observance of good faith.

2. Questions concerning matters governed by this Law which are not expressly settled in it are to be settled in conformity with the general principles on which this Law is based.

Article 4
Technology neutrality

Nothing in this Law requires the use of an automated system or a particular method in automated systems to form or perform contracts.

Article 5
Legal recognition of automated contracting

1. A contract formed using an automated system shall not be denied validity or enforceability on the sole ground that no natural person reviewed or intervened in any action carried out in connection with the formation of the contract.

[2. A contract performed using an automated system shall not be denied validity or enforceability on the sole ground that no natural person reviewed or intervened in any action carried out in connection with the performance of the contract.] [1]

3. An action carried out by an automated system in connection with the formation or performance of a contract shall not be denied legal effect, validity or enforceability on the sole ground that no natural person reviewed or intervened in the action.

Article 6
Legal recognition of contracts in computer code and use of dynamic information in automated contracting

1. A contract shall not be denied validity or enforceability on the sole ground that the terms of the contract are contained in data messages in the form of computer code.

2. A contract shall not be denied validity or enforceability on the sole ground that the terms of the contract incorporate information from a data source that provides information that changes periodically or continuously.

3. An action in connection with the formation of a contract shall not be denied legal effect, validity or enforceability on the sole ground that the action involves processing data messages containing information from a source that provides information that changes periodically or continuously.

Article 7
Attribution of actions carried out by automated systems

1. As between the parties to a contract, an action carried out by an automated system is attributed in accordance with a procedure agreed to by the parties.

2. If paragraph 1 does not apply, an action carried out by an automated system is attributed to the person who uses the system for that purpose.

3. Attribution of an action carried out by an automated system shall not be denied on the sole ground that the outcome was unexpected.

4. Nothing in this article affects the application of any rule of law that may govern the legal consequences of attributing an action carried out by an automated system to a person.

[**Article 8**
Unexpected actions carried out by automated systems

1. Unless otherwise agreed by the parties, where an action carried out by an automated system is attributed to a party to a contract, the other party to the contract is not entitled to rely on that action if, in the light of all the circumstances:

(a) The party to which the action is attributed could not reasonably have expected the action; and

(b) The other party knew or could reasonably be expected to have known that the party to which the action is attributed did not expect the action.

2. Nothing in this article affects the application of any rule of law or agreement of the parties that may govern the legal consequences of an action carried out by an automated system.][2]

[1] States that wish to extend the scope of article 5 to cover contracts that are performed using an automated system may wish to enact this provision.

[2] This provision is included for States wishing to enact one or more specific provisions addressing unexpected actions carried out by automated systems.

Article 9
Information requirements

Nothing in this Law affects the application of any rule of law that may require a person to disclose information on the design, operation or use of an automated system, or provides legal consequences for failing to do so or for disclosing inaccurate, incomplete or false information.

Article 10
Non-avoidance

Unless otherwise provided by law, a party shall not be relieved from the legal consequences of its failure to comply with a rule of law on the sole ground that it used an automated system.

Annex V

List of documents before the Commission at its fifty-seventh session

Symbol	*Title or description*
A/CN.9/1157/Rev.1	Provisional agenda, annotations thereto and scheduling of meetings of the fifty-seventh session
A/CN.9/1158	Report of Working Group I (Warehouse Receipts) on the work of its fortieth session
A/CN.9/1159	Report of Working Group II (Dispute Settlement) on the work of its seventy-eighth session
A/CN.9/1160	Report of Working Group III (Investor-State Dispute Settlement Reform) on the work of its forty-sixth session
A/CN.9/1161	Report of Working Group III (Investor-State Dispute Settlement Reform) on the work of its forty-seventh session
A/CN.9/1162	Report of Working Group IV (Electronic Commerce) on the work of its sixty-sixth session
A/CN.9/1163	Report of Working Group V (Insolvency Law) on the work of its sixty-third session
A/CN.9/1164	Report of Working Group VI (Negotiable Cargo Documents) on the work of its forty-third session
A/CN.9/1165	Report of Working Group I (Warehouse Receipts) on the work of its forty-first session
A/CN.9/1166	Report of Working Group II (Dispute Settlement) on the work of its seventy-ninth session
A/CN.9/1167	Report of Working Group III (Investor-State Dispute Settlement Reform) on the work of its forty-eighth session
A/CN.9/1169	Report of Working Group V (Insolvency Law) on the work of its sixty-fourth session
A/CN.9/1170	Report of Working Group VI (Negotiable Cargo Documents) on the work of its forty-fourth session
A/CN.9/1171	Bibliography of recent writings related to the work of UNCITRAL
A/CN.9/1172/Rev.1	Status of conventions and model laws and other UNCITRAL texts
A/CN.9/1173	Relevant General Assembly resolutions
A/CN.9/1174	Non-legislative activities
A/CN.9/1174/Add.1/Rev.1	Non-legislative activities – Technical cooperation and assistance

Symbol	*Title or description*
A/CN.9/1174/Add.2	Non-legislative activities – Activities of the UNCITRAL Regional Centre for Asia and the Pacific
A/CN.9/1174/Add.3	Non-legislative activities – Ways and means of ensuring a uniform interpretation and application of international conventions and uniform laws in the field of the law of international trade: CLOUT, digests and other materials
A/CN.9/1174/Add.4	Non-legislative activities – Operation of the transparency repository
A/CN.9/1174/Add.5	Non-legislative activities – UNCITRAL online and social media presence
A/CN.9/1174/Add.6	Non-legislative activities – UNCITRAL Law Library, publications, press releases and other outreach activities
A/CN.9/1174/Add.7	Non-legislative activities – Internship programme and moots
A/CN.9/1174/Add.8	Non-legislative activities – Planned activities for the period 1 January 2024 onwards
A/CN.9/1174/Add.9	Non-legislative activities – Resources and funding
A/CN.9/1175	Legal issues relating to the use of distributed ledger technology in trade
A/CN.9/1176	Coordination activities
A/CN.9/1177	Role of UNCITRAL in promoting the rule of law at the national and international levels
A/CN.9/1178	Draft provisions on automated contracting
A/CN.9/1179	Draft guide to enactment of the provisions on automated contracting
A/CN.9/1180	Work programme of the Commission
A/CN.9/1181	Draft UNCITRAL model clauses on specialized express dispute resolution
A/CN.9/1182	Draft model law on warehouse receipts
A/CN.9/1183	Draft guide to enactment of the UNCITRAL-UNIDROIT model law on warehouse receipts
A/CN.9/1184	Draft statute of an advisory centre on international investment dispute resolution
A/CN.9/1185	Possible reform of investor-State dispute settlement – Draft toolkit on prevention and mitigation of international investment disputes
A/CN.9/1186	Work Programme – Submission by the Governments of Germany, Israel, Japan, Republic of Korea and Spain

Symbol	Title or description
A/CN.9/1187	Coordination and cooperation – International governmental and non-governmental organizations invited to sessions of UNCITRAL and its working groups
A/CN.9/1188	Compilation of comments on the draft model law on warehouse receipts
A/CN.9/1188/Add.1	Compilation of comments on the draft model law on warehouse receipts
A/CN.9/1189	Stocktaking of developments in dispute resolution in the digital economy – progress report
A/CN.9/1190	Stocktaking of developments in dispute resolution in the digital economy – future work proposals
A/CN.9/1191	UNCITRAL-UNIDROIT study on the legal nature of verified carbon credits issued by independent carbon standard setters